English for All
Teil 1
Workbook

von Heinrich Schrand

 Ernst Klett Stuttgart

Herausgegeben von
Heinrich Schrand, Wissenschaftlicher Mitarbeiter und Landesprüfungsbeauftragter
für das Volkshochschul-Zertifikat Englisch in Hessen

1. Auflage $1^{5\ 4\ 3}$ | 1978 77 76

Alle Drucke dieser Auflage können im Unterricht nebeneinander benutzt werden. Die letzte
Zahl bezeichnet das Jahr dieses Druckes.
© Ernst Klett Verlag, Stuttgart 1974. Nach dem Urheberrechtsgesetz vom 9. Sept. 1965
i. d. F. vom 10. Nov. 1972 ist die Vervielfältigung oder Übertragung urheberrechtlich
geschützter Werke, also auch der Texte, Illustrationen und Graphiken dieses Buches, nicht
gestattet. Dieses Verbot erstreckt sich auch auf die Vervielfältigung für Zwecke der Unter-
richtsgestaltung — mit Ausnahme der in den §§ 53, 54 URG ausdrücklich genannten
Sonderfälle —, wenn nicht die Einwilligung des Verlages vorher eingeholt wurde. Im Einzel-
fall muß über die Zahlung einer Gebühr für die Nutzung fremden geistigen Eigentums
entschieden werden. Als Vervielfältigung gelten alle Verfahren einschließlich der Fotokopie,
der Übertragung auf Matrizen, der Speicherung auf Bändern, Platten, Transparenten oder
anderen Medien.
Einband: H. Lämmle, Stuttgart
Zeichnungen: H. Köhler, Stuttgart
Druck: Ernst Klett, 7 Stuttgart, Rotebühlstraße 77. Printed in Germany.
ISBN 3-12-524450-1

Contents

1 Welcome to England

1. Put in the right words

England, English, German, Germany, happy, holiday, invitation, station, way, Welcome

This is Helga.

She is in Berlin, in (1) . . . .

Is she (2) . . . .?

Yes, she is.

This is Robert.

He is in London, in (3) . . . .

Is he German?

No, he isn't, he is (4) . . . .

This is a letter.

Is it from Robert?

Yes, it is. It is an (5) . . . .

A (6) . . . . in England!

This is a ship.

Helga is on the ship.

She is on the (7) . . . . to England.

She is (8) . . . .

This is London.

Robert is at the (9) . . . .

Helga: "Hello, Robert!"

Robert: "Hello, Helga! (10) . . . . to England."

2. Look at the pictures and give short answers

1. Is Robert in London?

   Yes, he is.

2. Is Robert at the
   station?

   . . . .

3. Is Robert on an
   English ship?

   . . . .

4. Is Helga on the way to
   England?

   . . . .

5. Is Helga on an
   English ship?

   . . . .

6. Is Helga in Berlin?

   . . . .

3. Fill in the right questions

Is Helga German? Is Robert in Berlin? Is Robert English? Is the letter from Robert? Is Robert German?

Example:

Is Robert English?	Yes, he is.
1.	No, he isn't, he is English.
2.	Yes, she is.
3.	No, he isn't, he is in London.
4.	Yes, it is.

4. Give short answers

Examples:

Is Robert English?   Yes, he is.
Is Helga on the way to Germany?   No, she isn't.

1. Is Robert in London?   . . . .
2. Is Robert on a German ship?   . . . .
3. Is Helga on the way to England? . . . .
4. Is Robert at the station?   . . . .
5. Is the station in London?   . . . .
6. Is the letter from Helga?   . . . .
7. Is Helga English?   . . . .

5. Find the same sound

Example:

Robert is in London.

- ☐ a) Germany
- ☐ b) Berlin
- ☒ c) letter
- ☐ d) German

1. Helga is in Berlin, in Germany.

- ☐ a) Berlin
- ☐ b) Germany
- ☐ c) German
- ☐ d) welcome

2. Is the letter from Robert?

- ☐ a) not
- ☐ b) hello
- ☐ c) no
- ☐ d) London

3. Hello, Robert.

- ☐ a) from
- ☐ b) holiday
- ☐ c) no
- ☐ d) on

4. Is Helga on a German ship?

- ☐ a) Berlin
- ☐ b) Robert
- ☐ c) letter
- ☐ d) Germany

5. Welcome to England.

- ☐ a) way
- ☐ b) London
- ☐ c) station
- ☐ d) invitation

2 A Meal

1. Put in the right words

apples, butter, chips, cold, egg, fish, ham, hot, husband, meat, mother, plate, please, sardines, supper, vegetables, wife

It is a year later: Helga is Robert's (1) . . . .

Robert:	Hello, Helga! What's for (2) . . . . ? Steak and (3) . . . . ?
Helga:	No, Robert. But look, there are nice (4) . . . .
Robert:	No, thank you, Helga! No (5) . . . . ! What's that on the (6) . . . . ?
Helga:	That is cold (7) . . . . and beef.
Robert:	No, thank you, Helga! No cold (8) . . . .
Helga:	There's an (9) . . . ., there's salad and there are tomatoes.
Robert:	No, thank you. No eggs and no cold (10) . . . . What else is there?
Helga:	There's cheese, bread and (11) . . . ., there are oranges and (12) . . . . The apples are from my (13) . . . .
Robert:	No, no, Helga, not a (14) . . . . meal.
Helga:	What about a (15) . . . . German supper? There are sausages and sauerkraut.
Robert:	Yes, (16) . . . .! That's a nice German supper for a nice English (17) . . . . .

2

2. Give the answers

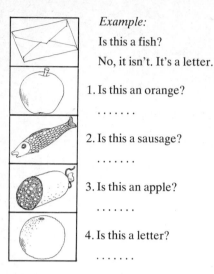

Example:
Is this a fish?
No, it isn't. It's a letter.

1. Is this an orange?
   . . . .

2. Is this a sausage?
   . . . .

3. Is this an apple?
   . . . .

4. Is this a letter?
   . . . .

3. Give the plurals

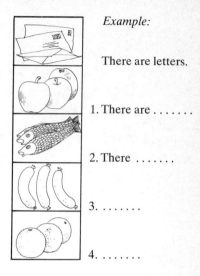

Example:

There are letters.

1. There are . . . .

2. There . . . .

3. . . . .

4. . . . .

4. Complete the sentences

Examples: There is a letter for Helga.
There are oranges on the plate.

1. . . . . a sausage for supper.
2. . . . . an egg on the plate.
3. . . . . tomatoes for supper.
4. . . . . an egg for Robert.

5. . . . . a letter for Robert.
6. . . . . eggs for Helga.
7. . . . . steaks for supper.
8. . . . . an apple on the plate.

5. Put in *a* or *an*

Examples: There's a letter from Robert.
There's an egg for Helga.

1. There's . . . . orange on the plate.
2. There's . . . . steak for Robert.
3. There's . . . . invitation for Helga.
4. There's . . . . apple for Robert.

5. There's . . . . hot sausage for Helga.
6. There's . . . . supper for Robert.
7. There's . . . . tomato for Helga.
8. There's . . . . nice husband for Helga.

6. Find the same sound

Example:

There's a hot **s**ausage for Helga.

- ☐ a) apples
- ☐ b) oranges
- ☒ c) **s**teaks
- ☐ d) tomatoes

1. There's a ni**c**e German supper for a ni**c**e English husband.

- ☐ a) tomatoes
- ☐ b) **s**upper
- ☐ c) oranges
- ☐ d) apples

2. There's an invitation for Helga.

- ☐ a) ham
- ☐ b) **s**tation
- ☐ c) **a**pple
- ☐ d) happy

3. There's **ch**eese.

- ☐ a) ve**g**etables
- ☐ b) **sh**ip
- ☐ c) **s**ausage
- ☐ d) **ch**ips

4. The orange is on the plate.

- ☐ a) the apple
- ☐ b) the station
- ☐ c) the plate
- ☐ d) the ship

5. The apples are from Germany.

- ☐ a) plates
- ☐ b) letters
- ☐ c) steaks
- ☐ d) stamps

6. The orange is on the plate.

- ☐ a) invitation
- ☐ b) salad
- ☐ c) apple
- ☐ d) orange

7. What's for supper?

- ☐ a) mother
- ☐ b) butter
- ☐ c) country
- ☐ d) holiday

3 The Car Keys

1. Put in the right words

bathroom, cupboard, dining-room, garden, girl, God, hall, hand, kitchen, late, living-room, moment, stop, upstairs, you

Mr and Mrs Brown are in the (1) . . . . It is time to go.

Mr Brown: Hurry up, Mary. We are (2) . . . . Where are the car keys?

Mrs Brown: On the television set, Roy.

Mr Brown: No, no. These are the (3) . . . . . . keys. Where is Jenny?

Mrs Brown: Jenny! Where are (4) . . . .?

Jenny: I'm in the (5) . . . ., Mother.

Mrs Brown: Where are Father's car keys? Look in the (6) . . . . Hurry.

Jenny: All right. No, they aren't here.

Mr Brown: Look in the (7) . . . .

Jenny: All right. No, they aren't here.

Mr Brown: Look (8) . . . . in the bathroom and the bedrooms.

Jenny: All right. Wait a (9) . . . .

Mrs Brown: Oh, Roy, we are late.

Mr Brown: We're always late in this house. Thank (10) . . . . there's a bus

(11) . . . . . . outside. Come on!

Jenny: Dad! Dad! There are keys in the (12) . . . .

Mr Brown: Good (13) . . . .! Hurry.

Jenny: Here, Dad. Are these the car keys?

Mr Brown: Oh no! Those are the (14) . . . . . . keys.

Jenny: But, Dad! What's that in your (15) . . . .?

Mr Brown: The car keys!

2. Fill in the right questions

Are the car keys in the hall? Are you from England? Is Jenny always late? Jenny! Where are you? Where are the garden keys? Where are Mr and Mrs Brown?

Example:

Are you from England?   No, I'm not.

1. . . . .   No, they aren't.

2. . . . .   I'm in the kitchen.

3. . . . .   They're in the living-room.

4. . . . .   No, she isn't.

5. . . . .   They're on the television set.

3. Give short answers

Examples:

Roy, are you in the living-room?   Yes, I am.
Is Mary in the kitchen?   No, she isn't.

1. Are you from Germany?   Yes, ...

2. Is Mary always late?   No, ...

3. Mary, are you in the kitchen?   Yes, ...

4. Are the keys on the television set?   No, ...

5. Is Roy in the garden?   Yes, ...

6. Is the key on the television set?   No, ...

7. Mary and Roy, are you in the kitchen?   Yes, ...

8. Are Mr and Mrs Brown in the dining-room?   No, ...

4. *This* **or** *these*

5. *That* **or** *those*

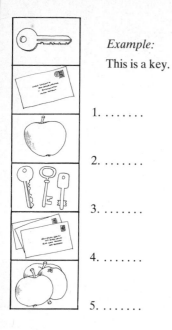

Example:

This is a key.

1. . . . .

2. . . . .

3. . . . .

4. . . . .

5. . . . .

Example:

That is a plate.

1. . . . .

2. . . . .

3. . . . .

4. . . . .

5. . . . .

6. Mark the correct answer with a cross ☒

Examples:

. . . . are on the television set.

☐ a) The key . . . .

☒ b) The keys . . . .

. . . . is in the living-room.

☒ a) He . . . .

☐ b) I . . . .

☐ c) They . . . .

1. . . . . is in the kitchen.

☐ a) She . . . .

☐ b) You . . . .

☐ c) I . . . .

2. . . . . are on the plate.

☐ a) The apple . . . .

☐ b) The apples . . . .

3. . . . . a letter for Roy.

☐ a) There is . . . .

☐ b) There are . . . .

4. . . . . is on the way to Germany.

☐ a) He . . . .

☐ b) We . . . .

☐ c) They . . . .

5. . . . . are upstairs.

- ☐ a) The bedroom . . . .
- ☐ b) The bedrooms . . . .

6. . . . . are in the garden.

- ☐ a) They . . . .
- ☐ b) She . . . .
- ☐ c) He . . . .

7. . . . . are happy.

- ☐ a) He . . . .
- ☐ b) They . . . .
- ☐ c) I . . . .

8. . . . . is a steak for Robert.

- ☐ a) This . . . .
- ☐ b) These . . . .

9. . . . . are English cars.

- ☐ a) That . . . .
- ☐ b) Those . . . .

10. . . . . aren't here.

- ☐ a) No, they . . . .
- ☐ b) The key . . . .
- ☐ c) There . . . .

7. Find the same sound

Example:

Robert is in London, in England.

- ☐ a) station
- ☐ b) invitation
- ☒ c) London
- ☐ d) way

1. Is Robert on a German ship?

- ☐ a) letter
- ☐ b) Germany
- ☐ c) Berlin
- ☐ d) Robert

2. Hello, Jenny.

- ☐ a) not
- ☐ b) Robert
- ☐ c) Roy
- ☐ d) those

3. The apples are on the plate.

- ☐ a) the orange
- ☐ b) the key
- ☐ c) the car
- ☐ d) the garden

4. These are keys, and those are plates.

- ☐ a) hands
- ☐ b) steaks
- ☐ c) plates
- ☐ d) stamps

5. Where are the plates?

- ☐ a) sardines
- ☐ b) vegetables
- ☐ c) eggs
- ☐ d) ships

4 At the Hotel

1. Put in the right words

address, another, bath, booked, call, double, guest, hall, help, key, kind, luggage, outside, pleasure, room, sorry, today, twin, wife

Here are Mr and Mrs Brown from Birmingham. They are in the hotel hall with their (1) . . . . . .

Hotel clerk:	Yes, sir?
Mr Brown:	A double room, please.
Clerk:	I'm (2) . . . ., sir, but we are full up. Our rooms are all (3) . . . .
Mr Brown:	Are they? Is there (4) . . . . hotel in this town?
Clerk:	No, sir. This is the only hotel here.
Mrs Brown:	Isn't there a (5) . . . . house in this town?
Clerk:	Yes, there is. My mother's guest house is only one mile from here. A nice (6) . . . . room is still free. Is your car (7) . . . ., sir?
Mr Brown:	Yes, it is.
Clerk:	My mother's house is very nice, sir. Here's her (8) . . . .
Mrs Brown:	Thank you very much. You're very (9) . . . .
Clerk:	It's a (10) . . . ., madam. Good-bye, sir. Good-bye, madam.

Twenty minutes later there is a phone (11) ....

Hotel clerk:	Ship Hotel. Good evening.
Clerk's mother:	Is that you, John? Mr Brown and his (12) .... are here. No more people (13) ...., John. I'm full up. Thank you for your (14) ......
Clerk:	All right, Mother.

An hour later. Mr and Mrs Smith from London are in the hotel (15) ....

Hotel clerk:	Good evening, madam. Good evening, sir.
Mr Smith:	Good evening. A double (16) ...., please.
Clerk:	Yes, sir. A double bed or (17) .... beds, sir?
Mr Smith:	Twin beds, please.
Clerk:	Very good, sir. With or without (18) ...., sir?
Mr Smith:	With bath, please.
Hotel clerk:	Here is your (19) ...., sir. Is your luggage outside, sir?

2. Give answers

Read the text on pages 20 and 21 of English for All, Part I, and answer the questions.

 Examples:

 Is Mr Smith from Birmingham?
 No, he isn't. He's from London.

 Is his wife from London?
 Yes, she is.

1. Is Mr Brown from London?

2. Is Mrs Brown from Birmingham?

3. Are Mr and Mrs Brown in the hotel hall?

4. Is their car outside the hotel?

5. Are they in the hotel hall with their luggage?

6. Is their luggage in their car?

7. Is the guest house one mile from the Ship Hotel?

3. Fill in the right questions

Are Mr and Mrs Smith in their room? Are you Mr and Mrs Brown? Is your luggage outside? Are you Mr Smith? Is there a guest house in this town? Where's the guest house?

Example:

Are you Mr Smith?   Yes, I am.

1. . . . .   Yes, it is.
2. . . . .   Yes, there is.
3. . . . .   It's one mile from here.
4. . . . .   Yes, we are.
5. . . . .   No, they aren't.

4. Ask questions and give answers

Example:

Peter
Is his name Peter? Yes, it is.

Helga/Jenny
Is her name Helga? No, it isn't, it's Jenny.

1. John/Robert   6. Helga
2. Jenny/Helga   7. Susan/Linda
3. Mary   8. Peter
4. Robert/John   9. Linda
5. Roy   10. Mary/Susan

5. Put in *from, in, on*

1. There's a guest house . . . . the town.
2. This is a letter . . . . Robert.
3. Jenny is . . . . the kitchen.
4. There are oranges . . . . the plate.
5. Mr Smith is . . . . London.
6. Helga is . . . . the ship.

6. Mark the correct answer with a cross ☒

Examples:

Mrs Brown: Roy, where are you? Here's . . . . supper.

☐ a) her   ☐ b) his   ☒ c) your

Roy: I'm upstairs in . . . . room.

☒ a) my   ☐ b) his

1. Mr and Mrs Smith are in the hotel hall. . . . . luggage is outside.

☐ a) His   ☐ b) Her   ☐ c) Their

2. *Roy:* Where are my keys? *Mary:* . . . . keys are in the hall.

☐ a) Their   ☐ b) Your

3. Mr Brown is in the hotel hall. . . . . car is outside.

☐ a) Her   ☐ b) His

4. Here's Mrs Smith. And where's . . . . luggage?

☐ a) his   ☐ b) her

5. *Robert:* Is that Jenny's car? *Mary:* Yes, that's . . . . . . car.

☐ a) her   ☐ b) his

6. *Hotel clerk:* Here's my mother's address. . . . . guest house is very nice.

☐ a) Her   ☐ b) His

7. This is Mr and Mrs Brown's house. . . . . rooms are nice.

☐ a) Its   ☐ b) His   ☐ c) Her

8. *Hotel clerk:* . . . . rooms are all booked. I'm very sorry.

☐ a) Your   ☐ b) Our

9. Thank you for . . . . help.

☐ a) my   ☐ b) your

10. Mr Brown and . . . . wife are here.

☐ a) his   ☐ b) her

5 Mr Brown's Birthday or the English Weather

1. Put in the right words

another, big, birthday, children, first, girl, Guess, guests, Happy, How, kisses, lighter, me, postman, present, raincoat, rainy, ring, sister, umbrella, you

Today is Mr Brown's (1) . . . . What is his wife's present?

She has a nice (2) . . . . for him. There's a ring at the door.

It's the (3) . . . . .He has a (4) . . . . parcel for Mr Brown. The parcel is full of German sausages. It is a (5) . . . . from his daughter in Germany.

"How nice of her," says Mr Brown. "She's very good to us."

There is another (6) . . . at the door. It's Robert and Helga. They are the (7) . . . guests.

"(8) . . . . birthday, Roy!"

They have presents for him. Robert has a nice cigarette–(9) . . . ., Helga an umbrella. There are more (10) . . . .: the Smiths with their (11) . . . ., a boy and a (12) . . . . Then there are the neighbours. They all have presents for Mr Brown. Four of them are umbrellas. Mr Brown is very happy.

"Thank you, thank you! (13) . . . . nice of you. Are all those umbrellas for

(14) . . . .? I've got enough now for six (15) . . . . days. What about a drink? Whisky, gin?"

The gentlemen have whisky, the ladies gin.

There is another ring. It is Mr Brown's (16) . . . ., Joy.

"Hello, Roy! Here is a nice present for you from me: two big (17) . . . ."

"You're a nice woman, Joy. And a kiss from (18) . . . . is a nice present. But is that all? Haven't you got (19) . . . . present for me?"

"Yes, Roy, my boy. (20) . . . .!"

"An umbrella!" – "No, a (21) . . . .!"

2. Give the answers to these questions

Examples:

Where's the butter? (table)
It's on the table.

Where are Mr and Mrs Brown? (hotel hall)
They're in the hotel hall.

1. Where's the apple? (plate)
2. Where's the parcel? (table)
3. Where's Jenny? (kitchen)

4. Where are the car keys? (his hand)
5. Where's Mr Smith? (garden)
6. Where are the letters? (television set)

**Kreisvolkshochschule
Main-Kinzig
645 Hanau**, Eugen-Kaiser-Str. 10

3. Give short answers

Examples:

Have you got a sister?	Yes, I have.
Has your mother got a car?	No, she hasn't.

1. Have Robert and Helga got presents for Mr Brown?   Yes, ...
2. Have you got a car?   No, ...
3. Have your neighbours got a car?   Yes, ...
4. Have you got a garden?   Yes, ...
5. Have your neighbours got a garden?   No, ...
6. Has Roy got a car?   No, ...
7. Have the Browns got a house?   Yes, ...
8. Have your neighbours got a television set?   No, ...

5

4. Ask questions and give answers

Examples

(you/sister) (yes)
Have you got a sister? Yes, I have.

(Roy/car) (no)
Has Roy got a car? No, he hasn't.

1. (you/raincoat) (no)
2. (Helga/umbrella) (yes)
3. (you/cigarette-lighter) (yes)
4. (your neighbours/television set) (no)
5. (the Smiths/two children) (yes)
6. (they/garden) (yes)

5. Mark the correct answer with a cross ☒

Example:

The Browns . . . . a big house.
☒ a) have ☐ b) has

1. On her birthday Mrs Smith . . . . guests.
☐ a) have ☐ b) has

2. The guests . . . . presents for her.
☐ a) have ☐ b) has

3. Robert . . . . a nice cigarette-lighter for Mrs Smith.
☐ a) have ☐ b) has

4. Hello, John, here's a letter for . . . .
☐ a) him ☐ b) you

5. Where are the girls? Here's gin for . . . .
☐ a) her ☐ b) them

6. This is a letter . . . . is for Robert.
☐ a) It ☐ b) He

7. Where's the key? . . . . on the television set.
☐ a) It's ☐ b) He's

8. Where's the butter? . . . . on the table.
☐ a) It's ☐ b) She's

9. Today is Joy's birthday, and the guests have got nice presents for . . . .
☐ a) her ☐ b) them

6 Spell it, please!

1. Put in the right words

bears, beer, chickens, figs, grapes, hams, Herrings, line, noodles, order, pears, phone, pigs, present, quality, raincoat, sauerkraut, sheep, tins

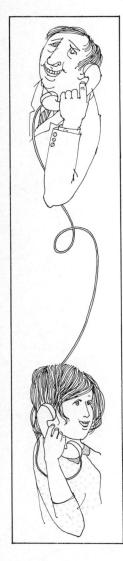

Mr Spencer is on the (1) . . . . to Hamburg.

Spencer: Hello, Hamburg? This is Spencers Continental Food Import, London. Here's my (2) . . . . : Fifteen pounds of fish.

Woman's Voice: What fish, please?

Spencer: (3) . . . . – And a thousand young chickens.

Voice: How many (4) . . . . , sir?

Spencer: A thousand. – And a box of (5) . . . .

Voice: An ox and (6) . . . .

Spencer: What is the (7) . . . . of your pears?

Voice: We have very good (8) . . . . , sir.

Spencer: All right! Twenty-eight boxes of (9) . . . .

Voice: Twenty-eight bears.

Spencer: Five hundred and fifty bottles of German (10) . . . .

Voice: German deer?

Spencer: Yes, dear, German. – And two hundred and forty pounds of (11) . . . .

Voice: Two hundred and forty poodles.

Spencer: And twelve boxes of (12) . . . .

Voice: Twelve apes.

Spencer: No. Grapes.

Voice: Spell it, please. The (13) . . . . is not clear.

Spencer: Grapes! 'G' for 'garden', 'r' for (14) '. . . . . . . ', 'a' for 'apple', 'p' for (15) '. . . . . . . ', 'e' for 'egg', 's' for 'salad'. And forty-nine cheap (16) . . . .

Voice: Forty-nine (17) . . . . and lambs.

Spencer: And two thousand (18) . . . . of sauerkraut.

Voice: What? Sauerkraut?

Spencer: Yes, sauerkraut: s–a–u–e–r–k–r–a–u–t!

Haven't you got two thousand tins of sauerkraut?

Voice: We have no (19) . . . ., sir.

Spencer: No sauerkraut? Aren't you Schmitz Lebensmittel-Export?

Voice: No, we're not. This is Hagenbeck's Tierhandel.

2. Fill in the right questions

Is his name John? What's her name? Is her name Mary? What's your name? What's his name? What's your address?

Example:

Is his name John?   No, it isn't.

1. . . . .   His name is Roy.

2. . . . .   My name is Jenny.

3. . . . .   My address is 2, King Street.

4. . . . .   No, it isn't.

5. . . . .   Her name is Joy.

3. Write the numbers

Example:

5 pears   five

1. 20 girls	. . . .	6. 9 raincoats	. . . .
2. 6 bottles	. . . .	7. 2 eggs	. . . .
3. 8 umbrellas	. . . .	8. 15 oranges	. . . .
4. 12 boxes	. . . .	9. 19 apples	. . . .
5. 4 cars	. . . .	10. 11 parcels	. . . .

4. Answer the questions

Example:

How many keys are there on the television set? (1/3)
There is one key on the television set.
There are three keys on the television set.

1. How many oranges are there on the plate? (2/4)

2. How many apples are there on the table? (1/5)

3. How many girls are there at the bus stop? (1/6)

4. How many parcels are there in the cupboard? (3/8)

5. Mark the correct answer with a cross ☒

Examples:

. . . . is in the dining-room.
☐ a) I   ☒ b) He   ☐ c) We

Is Robert . . . . a German ship? No, he isn't.
☒ a) on   ☐ b) at

1. Is the station in London? Yes, ... is.
☐ a) he   ☐ b) it

2. . . . . a letter for Roy.
☐ a) There is   ☐ b) There are

3. . . . . are in the hotel hall.
☐ a) He   ☐ b) They   ☐ c) She

4. . . . . is on the way to Germany.
☐ a) She   ☐ b) They   ☐ c) I

5. There's . . . . apple for John.
☐ a) an   ☐ b) a

6. What's . . . . that plate? That is cold ham and beef.
☐ a) in   ☐ b) on

7. There's a gentleman . . . . the bus stop.
☐ a) at   ☐ b) on

8. John and Mary are in the hotel hall. . . . . luggage is outside.
☐ a) His   ☐ b) Her   ☐ c) Their

9. The Smiths . . . . a big house.
☐ a) have   ☐ b) has

10. Today is Mary's birthday, and the guests have got nice presents for . . . .
☐ a) them   ☐ b) her

11. Is this the . . . . car? Yes, it is.
☐ a) Browns'   ☐ b) Brown's

7 The Broken Lamp

1. Put in the right words

Answer, bedroom, beside, broken, for, helping, living-room, Lock, locked, man, neighbour, police, ring, speaking, together, upstairs, watching

Robert and Helga are watching TV. There's a (1) . . . . It's the phone.

Helga: The phone is ringing, Robert. (2) . . . . it, please.

Robert: Hello? Who's (3) . . . .?–It's Vivien, their (4) . . . .

Robert: Yes, Vivien? Aren't you (5) . . . . TV? There's a good film on.

Vivien: Robert, a man is moving (6) . . . . in my bedroom. I'm phoning from the (7) . . . . now.

Robert: (8) . . . . the door.

Vivien: The door is (9) . . . . Please, Robert, come and help me.

Robert: All right. Wait (10) . . . . me. I'm coming.

Helga: Where are you going, Robert?

Robert: I'm going to Vivien's house. There's a (11) . . . . in her room upstairs.

Helga: Let's go (12) . . . .

Robert: No, stay here. Phone the police.

Four minutes later: Robert is in Vivien's house. A (13) . . . . car is coming.

Policeman: What are you doing there?

Robert: I'm (14) . . . . a neighbour. There's a man in her (15) . . . .

The policemen are soon upstairs. There is a (16) . . . . lamp on the floor. A big cat is sitting (17) . . . . it.

2. Fill in the right questions

Is your name Mary? How are you? Has Jenny got a phone? What's your name? Where's John? Where's my raincoat? Is this your lighter? What's her number? How is he today?

Example:

Is your name Mary?   No, it isn't.

1. . . . .   My name's Vivien.

2. . . . .   I'm very well, thank you.

3. . . . .   He's in the house.

4. . . . .   He's feeling fine.

5. . . . .   Yes, that's my lighter.

6. . . . .   It's on the floor.

7. . . . .   Yes, she has.

8. . . . .   Her number is 351 9338.

3. Put in *what, where, who*

Example:

Where are the car keys?   On the television set.

1. . . . . are you doing there? I'm helping a neighbour.

2. . . . . are you going, John? I'm going to Mary's house.

3. . . . . is your address?   My address is 5, Garden Street.

4. . . . . is in the kitchen?   Jenny is.

5. Jenny! . . . . are you?   I'm in the kitchen.

6. . . . . is that on the plate? That is cold ham and beef.

4. Questions and answers

Example:

(Robert) (sit/living-room)

What is Robert doing?

He is sitting in the living-room.

1. (Robert)
   (sit/living-room)

2. (Helga)
   (watch/TV)

3. (Vivien)
   (phone/Robert)

4. (Robert)
   (go/to Vivien's house)

5. (policeman)
   (watch/Robert)

6. (cat)
   (sit/floor)

7. (Robert and Helga)
   (wait/bus stop)

8. (Robert and Helga)
   (hurry/station)

9. (Robert and Helga)
   (go/Germany)

10. (Mr and Mrs Brown)
    (look/their car)

11. (the Browns)
    (go/their house)

12. (the Browns)
    (watch/TV)

5. Ask questions and give answers

Example:

the children/wait at the bus stop
What are the children doing?
They're waiting at the bus stop.

1. Joy/watch TV
2. Robert/phone the police
3. the children/help a neighbour

4. the policeman/watch John
5. the girl/sit on the floor
6. the boys/hurry to the station

6. Ask questions and give answers

Example:

Robert and Helga/have supper/watch TV
What are Robert and Helga doing? Are they having supper?
No, they aren't. They are watching TV.

1. Robert/call the police/answer the phone
2. Vivien/watch TV/phone from the living-room
3. man/ring at the door/move upstairs
4. Helga/lock the door/phone the police
5. policeman/watch the house/hurry upstairs
6. cat/have a meal/sit on the floor

8 In the Lift

1. Put in the right words

button, evening, fifth, floor, for, happens, holds, idea, lady, lift, name, Press, reaches,
rings, sixth, spoilt, stops, stuck, theatre, third, ticket, Wait

A young man is waiting (1) . . . . the lift on the tenth floor of a big hotel. The lift
comes, and the man gets in.

A woman's voice: (2) . . . . for me!

The man (3) . . . . the door open, and a young (4) . . . . gets in.

He: Ground floor?
She: Yes, please.

The (5) . . . . . . goes down. Ninth (6) . . . ., eighth, seventh, (7) . . . .
The lift (8) . . . .

She: What's the matter?
He: We're (9) . . . .
She: Oh, how awful! I have a (10) . . . . for a concert at eight o'clock.
He: And I have a ticket for the (11) . . . .!

She: Please do something. (12) . . . . the alarm button.

The alarm (13) . . . . and a man's voice shouts from below: "What's the matter?"

He: We're stuck between the (14) . . . . and the sixth.

Man's voice: That (15) . . . . every day. Give me five minutes.

Five minutes, ten minutes, thirty minutes! They are still in the lift.

She: It's ten past eight. My evening is (16) . . . .

He: Never mind. Let's make the best of it. My (17) . . . . is John Blake.

She: And my name is Kate Winter.

Man's voice from below: Press the (18) . . . . It's all right now.

John presses the button and the lift goes down. Fifth floor, fourth, (19) . . . ., second, first. The lift (20) . . . . the ground floor, and Kate and John get out.

John: At last! What can we do with the rest of the (21) . . . .?

What about a drink in the bar, Kate?

Kate: That's a nice (22) . . . ., John. Thank you very much.

2. Put in *at, for, in, on, to*

1. Jenny, where are you? I'm upstairs . . . . my room.
2. Wait . . . . me. I'm coming.
3. There's a broken lamp . . . . the floor.
4. I have a ticket for a concert . . . . eight o'clock.
5. Where are you going, John? I'm going . . . . Mary's house.

3. Put in the right form of *go, help, wait, watch*

1. Kate . . . . at the bus stop every day.
2. Roy and Mary . . . . television every evening.
3. Mr Smith . . . . his wife in the kitchen every day.
4. The children . . . . at the station every day.
5. John . . . . to Birmingham every day.
6. Mrs Brown . . . . TV every evening.
7. They . . . . the neighbours every day.
8. Tom and Joy . . . . to London every day.

4. Mark the correct answer with a cross ☒

Example:

Mr Smith says, I . . . . to London every day.
☐ a) am going ☒ b) go ☐ c) goes

1. Kate and John are happy now. They . . . . a drink at the bar.
   ☐ a) have ☐ b) are having ☐ c) has

2. Let's go to the cinema.– No, I . . . . TV.
   ☐ a) am watching ☐ b) watch ☐ c) watches

3. Tom . . . . Vivien in the garden every day.
   ☐ a) help ☐ b) helps ☐ c) is helping

4. Look. Robert . . . . for Helga.
   ☐ a) waits ☐ b) is waiting ☐ c) wait

5. They . . . . whisky every day.
   ☐ a) are drinking ☐ b) drink ☐ c) drinks

6. Look. A police car . . . .
   ☐ a) is coming ☐ b) comes ☐ c) come

5. Find the same sound

Example:

Mr Brown goes to London every day.
☐ a) waits ☐ b) drinks ☐ c) helps ☒ d) holds

1. John waits at the bus stop every day.
   ☐ a) locks ☐ b) phones ☐ c) comes ☐ d) stays

2. Mary phones her mother every day.
   ☐ a) sits ☐ b) gets ☐ c) says ☐ d) speaks

3. Joy watches TV every evening.
   ☐ a) moves ☐ b) phones ☐ c) goes ☐ d) reaches

4. Robert answers the phone every day.
   ☐ a) gives ☐ b) locks ☐ c) waits ☐ d) helps

5. Mr Brown hurries to the station every day.
   ☐ a) drinks ☐ b) looks ☐ c) stays ☐ d) sits

9 A Date

1. Put in the right words

addresses, already, at, clock, date, disappears, hairdresser's, hour, late, leaves, lend,
minutes, past, quarter, quarters, set, statue, surprise, terrible, time, waits, watch, wig

It is half past three. Kate enters the (1) . . . .

"A shampoo and a (2) . . . . . .," she says.

"Yes, madam," says the hairdresser. "Please come this way."

He gives Kate a chair. Four ladies are (3) . . . . waiting.

"But I've a (4) . . . . at five o'clock," says Kate.

"Yes, madam," says the hairdresser. "That's all right."

Kate waits and (5) . . . .

Half an (6) . . . . later she calls the hairdresser.

"It's four o'clock!"

"Yes, madam. I'm doing my best. Only another five (7) . . . ., please."

At a (8) . . . . to five Kate calls the hairdresser again.

"It's too (9) . . . . now. Look (10) . . . . my hair. What can I do?"

"We can (11) . . . . you a wig, madam. Here is a nice blond (12) . . . . Try it on."

Kate tries it on. Her dark hair (13) . . . . under the blond wig.

"That's very nice," says Kate. "Thank you so much."

She (14) . . . . the hairdresser's at five o'clock and reaches Piccadilly Circus three (15) . . . . of an hour later.

John's taxi reaches Piccadilly Circus at a quarter (16) . . . . five.

John hurries to the Eros Statue. A lot of people are waiting under the (17) . . . ., but Kate is not there.

A quarter of an hour later John looks at the big Guiness (18) . . . .

The time is half past five. Kate is late. What a (19) . . . . girl!

At a quarter to six John looks at his (20) . . . . again. He is tired and hungry.

At ten to six a blond girl (21) . . . . him with a smile. "Excuse me. What's the (22) . . . . by your watch?"

John looks at his watch. Then he looks at the blond girl. Suddenly he laughs. What a (23) . . . .! The girl is Kate.

2. What's the time?

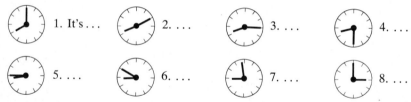

1. It's . . .   2. . . .   3. . . .   4. . . .

5. . . .   6. . . .   7. . . .   8. . . .

And what's the time by your watch?

3. Ask questions and give answers

Example:

Oxford / my father / 8:30

Where are you going? – I'm going to Oxford.
Who's going with you? – My father is.
When are you going? – At half past eight.

1. Berlin / my sister / 11:20
2. London / my wife / 10:45
3. Birmingham / my mother / 9:15
4. Glasgow / my daughter / 9:55
5. Germany / my husband / 8:45

4. Form sentences

Example:

7.30 / John and Kate / in the lift
At half past seven John and Kate are in the lift.

1. 8.10 / John and Kate / still in the lift

2. 8.15 / a voice / "Press the button."

3. 8.30 / they / a drink in the bar

4. 10.45 / they / still in the bar

5. 11.00 / they / in the lift again

5. Find the same sound

Mark the words which contain the same sound as the underlined word.

Tom watch<u>es</u> TV every evening.

☐ a) phones   ☐ d) goes   ☐ g) brushes

☐ b) comes   ☐ e) presses   ☐ h) washes

☐ c) reaches   ☐ f) gives   ☐ i) leaves

6. Put in the right form

1. (enter)   At half past three Kate . . . . the hairdresser's.

2. (give)   The hairdresser . . . . Kate a chair.

3. (wait)   Four ladies . . . .

4. (call)   Half an hour later Kate . . . . the hairdresser.

5. (do)   "Only another five minutes, please," he says, "I . . . . my best".

6. (leave)   It is too late. At five o'clock Kate . . . . the hairdresser's.

7. (hurry)   She . . . . to the Eros Statue at Picadilly Circus.

8. (wait)   A lot of people . . . . under the statue.

9. (do)   What is Kate . . . . now?

10. (address) She . . . . John with a smile. They are laughing.

10 Reporter Jack Quick and the Football Player

1. Put in the right words

answering, drink, drinking, favourite, giving, having, page, pipe, play, playing, questions, read, reading, reporter, Saturday, sitting, smoke, smoking, Sunday, train, watch, watching

Jack Quick is a newspaper (1) . . . . He is asking Freddie Brown (2) . . . .

Is your training very hard,
Freddie?
    Yes, it is.
    I (3) . . . . four or five
    hours every day.

Is Freddie training
at the moment?
No, he isn't.
He is (14) . . . .
on a chair.

You play every (4) . . . .?
    Yes, I (5) . . . .
    every Saturday.
    But I never play
    on (6) . . . .

Is Freddie (15) . . . . .
football now?
No, he isn't.
He is (16) . . . .
questions.

You (7) . . . . newspapers
every day,
Freddie?
    Yes, I always read
    the sports (8) . . . .

Is Freddie (17) . . . . .
now?
No, he isn't.
He is playing
with a football.

What is your (9) . . . . drink,
Freddie? Whisky, beer?
    I seldom (10) . . . . . . whisky,
    but I often drink
    a glass of beer.

Is Freddie (18) . . . . .
whisky at
the moment?
No, he isn't.
He is (19) . . . . . . tea.

What are your favourite
cigarettes?
    I never (11) . . . . . cigarettes.
    I sometimes smoke a (12) . . . .

Is he (20) . . . . . now?
Yes, he is.
He is smoking
a pipe.

Have you got a hobby,
Freddie?
    Yes, I often (13) . . . .
    football on TV.
Thank you very much,
Freddie. Good-bye.

Is he (21) . . . .
TV now?
No, he isn't.
He is (22) . . . .
Mr Quick
an interview.

2. Form sentences

Example:

(often – to the theatre – go)
Freddie often goes to the theatre.

1. (leave – his house at 8.00 – always)
2. (at 10.00 – answer – the reporter's questions)
3. (very hard – in the evening – train)
4. (a glass of beer – drink – often)
5. (always – the sports page – read)
6. (smoke – sometimes – a pipe)
7. (every evening – at 7.30 – have supper)
8. (watch – football on TV – often)

Kreisvolkshochschule
Main-Kinzig
645 Hanau, Eugen-Kaiser-Str. 10

3. Form sentences

Example:

goes to a pub/he/in the evening/often
He often goes to a pub in the evening.

1. reads the newspaper/Robert/in the evening/always
2. play football/the boys/on Saturdays/often
3. leaves the house/he/at six o'clock/sometimes
4. helps his wife/he/in the kitchen/seldom
5. smokes a pipe/Robert/after supper/always
6. drinks whisky/Tom/never/in the morning

4. Opposites

never, get out, evening, wife, answer, seldom, boy, mother, go

Example:

sister	–	brother		5. father	. . . .
1. come	. . . .			6. girl	. . . .
2. husband	. . . .			7. get in	. . . .
3. always	. . . .			8. often	. . . .
4. question	. . . .			9. morning	. . . .

5. Mark the correct answer with a cross ☒

Example:

Freddie . . . . for four or five hours every day.

☐ a) is training ☒ b) trains ☐ c) train

1. He never . . . . on Sundays.

☐ a) is training ☐ b) train ☐ c) trains

2. Look, Freddie . . . . football.

☐ a) plays ☐ b) is playing ☐ c) play

3. Peter . . . . football on TV.

☐ a) watches often ☐ b) often watches ☐ c) is often watching

4. Father sometimes . . . . a pipe after supper.

☐ a) is smoking ☐ b) smoke ☐ c) smokes

5. Look, Mary . . . . a pipe.

☐ a) is smoking ☐ b) smokes ☐ c) smoke

6. What's Jack doing? He . . . . Freddie.

☐ a) phones ☐ b) is phoning ☐ c) phone

7. Robert . . . . the sports page of the newspaper.

☐ a) reads always ☐ b) always is reading ☐ c) always reads

11 The Third Man's Story

1. Put in the right words

arrive, begins, can, cannot, downstairs, end, floor, gentlemen, ground, hungry, lift, meal, must, restaurant, short, single, start, tell, turn, until, walk

Three men (1) . . . . at a New York hotel near the Empire State Building. It is late in the evening and they are tired and (2) . . . .

"Can we have three (3) . . . . rooms?" they ask the hotel clerk.

"I can give you three single rooms on the forty-third (4) . . . ., but I must tell you that you can't use the (5) . . . . . . It's out of order. You must (6) . . . . . up."

"Walk up? Can't you give us three rooms on the tenth floor?"

"No, I can't. We're full up. Take the rooms, (7) . . . . The other hotels must be full up, too."

"Is there a (8) . . . . in the hotel where we can have a (9) . . . .? We want to have a meal before we (10) . . . . . .," says one of the men.

"There's a restaurant here on the (11) . . . . floor. May I show you the way?"

After their meal the men walk up.

"Can't we (12) . . . . each other stories?" says one of the men. "It's a long way to the forty-third. George, can you start?"

The first man (13) . . . . to tell his story. It is rather long, and when it comes to an (14) . . . ., they are already on the fourteenth floor. Then the second man (15) . . . . . . tell his story. It lasts (16) . . . . they reach the thirty-first floor. It is the third man's (17) . . . . now. He stops, opens his mouth, but he (18) . . . . say a word.

"What's the matter?" ask the other two. "Can't you think of a story?" The third man (19) . . . ., but he says, "Must I tell it?"

"Yes, you must," say the other two.

"My story is very (20) . . . . and very sad," says the third man. "The keys of our rooms are still (21) . . . . at the clerk's desk."

2. Questions and answers

Example:

1. Good morning, Jack. – j) Good morning, Robert.

1. Good morning, Jack.	a) I'm watching TV.
2. How are you?	b) She's in the living-room.
3. What are you doing now?	c) I'm very well, thank you.
4. What's this?	d) It's a cigarette-lighter.
5. Is this your umbrella?	e) It's on the bed.
6. Where's the raincoat?	f) Yes, that's my umbrella.
7. Where's Mary?	g) No, they aren't.
8. Are Mary and Kate sisters?	h) His name is Freddie.
9. What's the man's name?	i) Yes, he is.
10. Is he a newspaper reporter?	j) Good morning, Robert.

3. Addresses

These people live in England. Write their addresses.

Example:

Mr Roy Brown lives in London, SE192NT.
He lives at 146 Church Street.

Mr Roy Brown
146 Church Street
London, SE192NT
England

1. Miss Kate Winter lives in Folkestone, Kent.
   She lives at 25 Grimston Gardens.
2. Mr Jack Quick lives in London, W1V 8HJ.
   He lives at 40 Shaftesbury Avenue.
3. Mr and Mrs Robert Smith live in Hove, Sussex.
   They live at 33 Palmeira Mansions.
4. Mr John Blake lives in Poole, Dorset.
   He lives at 14 Durlston Road.

4. Give short answers

Examples:

Can you help me?	Yes, I can.
May I phone Kate?	No, you may not.

1. Can you and Robert answer this question?   No, ...

2. Must I tell you the story?   Yes, ...

3. Can Tom answer the phone in English?   Yes, ...

4. Can your wife read an English newspaper?   No, ...

5. Must the boys hurry?   Yes, ...

6. May we smoke in here?   No, ...

7. May we come to your party?   Yes, ...

8. May Mary come?   No, ...

9. Can John read this book?   No, ...

5. Fill in the right questions

Can she play football? Must the men walk up? May John watch TV? May I have a glass of beer? Can you play tennis? Can we have a double room?

Example:

Can she play football?	Yes, she can.

1. . . . .   Yes, you may.

2. . . . .   No, you can't.

3. . . . .   Yes, they must.

4. . . . .   Yes, I can.

5. . . . .   No, he may not.

6. Mark the correct answer with a cross ☒

Example:

What's . . . . name? My name is Helga.

☐ a) her   ☒ b) your

1. I can go to the dance, but you . . . .

     ☐ a) can't   ☐ b) can

2. What's Mary doing? She . . . . for her husband.

☐ a) is waiting   ☐ b) waits

3. Tom . . . .

☐ a) can the story tell.   ☐ b) can tell the story.

4. Can Tom play football? Yes. He . . . . football now.

☐ a) is playing   ☐ b) plays

5. These people can't come, but those people . . . .

☐ a) can't.   ☐ b) can.

6. . . . . Mary? She's in the kitchen.

☐ a) Who's   ☐ b) Where's

7. We must . . . .

☐ a) phone Mr Brown.   ☐ b) Mr Brown phone.

8. May I use Father's car? Yes, you . . . .

☐ a) may not.   ☐ b) may.

9. May I . . . .?

☐ a) have an apple   ☐ b) an apple have

10. . . . . a double room? – No, you can't.

☐ a) Can I have   ☐ b) I want

11. . . . . a double room free? – I'm sorry, but I haven't.

☐ a) Have you got   ☐ b) Can I have

12. She can . . . .

☐ a) you the room show.   ☐ b) show you the room.

13. Is there a hotel where . . . . a meal?

☐ a) can we have   ☐ b) we can have

14. I always . . . . my wife in the kitchen.

☐ a) help   ☐ b) am helping

12 Are You the Perfect Husband?

1. Put in the right words

*always, answers, ask, boss, car, doctor, drive, friend, help, her, home, liar, lucky,
never, notice, office, on, play, spend, take, washing, welcome*

1. a) Do you give your wife a cup of tea in bed every morning?

   b) Do you give your wife a cup of tea in bed (1) . . . . Sundays?

   c) Do you (2) . . . . give your wife a cup of tea in bed?

2. a) Do you sometimes play the (3) . . . .?

   b) Do you (4) . . . . play the boss?

   c) Do you never (5) . . . . the boss?

3. a) Do you never (6) . . . . your wife in the house?

   b) Do you sometimes help (7) . . . .?

   c) Do you always help her?

4. Your wife is out when you come (8) . . . . in the evening.

   a) Do you do the (9) . . . . up?

   b) Do you (10) . . . . a lot of questions when she comes home?

   c) Do you go out, too?

5. Your wife has a cold.

   a) Do you (11) . . . . no notice?

   b) Do you ask her whether she wants a (12) . . . .?

   c) Do you say, "Keep away from me"?

6. Do you (13) . . . . your holidays

   a) alone?

   b) with your wife?

   c) with a (14) . . . .?

7. a) Does your wife sometimes (15) . . . . your car?

   b) Does your wife never drive your (16) . . . .?

   b) Does your wife always drive your car?   c)

8. You come home from the (17) . . . . in the evening.

   a) Does your wife (18) . . . . you with a kiss?

   b) Does she take no (19) . . . . of you?

   c) Does she say, "Take your shoes off at the front door"?

You get ten points for each of the following (20) . . . .:

1a, 2c, 3c, 4a, 5b, 6b, 7a, 8a.

Under forty points:	Your wife is not very (21) . . . .
Forty points or more:	Your wife must be very nice.
Eighty points:	You are the perfect husband or the perfect (22) . . . ., sir.

2. Questions and answers

   Example:

   1. Hello, Tom. – i) Hello, Robert.

1. Hello, Tom.	a) I'm very well, thank you.
2. How are you?	b) Yes, he is.
3. Do you like tennis?	c) Yes, I can.
4. Can you play football?	d) Yes, I do.
5. Is your brother a policeman?	e) Yes, she does.
6. Does he like football?	f) I smoke cigarettes.
7. Does your sister live in Birmingham?	g) He smokes a pipe.
8. What do you smoke?	h) Yes, he does.
9. What does your brother smoke?	i) Hello, Robert.

3. Form new sentences

Example:

Look, Mary is drinking beer. (often)
She often drinks beer.

1. Look, Tom is reading the newspaper. (seldom)
2. Look, Kate is washing the car. (sometimes)
3. Look, the boys and girls are dancing. (often)
4. Look, Freddie is playing football. (never)
5. Look, the children are playing tennis. (sometimes)
6. Look, Vivien is smoking a pipe. (never)
7. Look, Helga is drinking whisky. (seldom)

4. Give short answers

Examples:

Does Freddie leave the house at six o'clock?   Yes, he does.
Does Tom play football on Sundays?   No, he doesn't.

1. Does Mr Smith smoke a cigarette after supper?   No, ...
2. Do Tom and Mary play tennis on Saturdays?   Yes, ...
3. Do the children go to bed at eight o'clock?   No, ...
4. Does Mary clean the floors in the morning?   No, ...
5. Does Tom walk to the office?   Yes, ...
6. Does Kate arrive at the office at seven o'clock?   Yes, ...
7. Does Mrs Brown smoke a cigarette after dinner?   No, ...
8. Do your sisters get up late?   Yes, ...

5. Mark the correct answer with a cross ☒

Example:

What . . . .?

☐ a) the perfect husband do
☒ b) does the perfect husband do
☐ c) does the perfect husband

1. Does your husband . . . . a cup of tea in bed?

   ☐ a) give you always

   ☐ b) always give you

   ☐ c) give always you

2. Does Robert smoke?

   ☐ a) No, he does.

   ☐ b) No, he doesn't.

   ☐ c) Yes, he doesn't.

3. When . . . . your house in the morning?

   ☐ a) do you leave

   ☐ b) leave you

   ☐ c) you leave

4. Does Tom's sister often drink whisky?

   ☐ a) Yes, he does.

   ☐ b) No, he doesn't.

   ☐ c) No, she doesn't.

5. What . . . . on Sundays?

   ☐ a) Freddie does

   ☐ b) does Freddie do

   ☐ c) does Freddie

6. Does your wife . . . . a car?

   ☐ a) drive sometimes

   ☐ b) sometimes drives

   ☐ c) sometimes drive

7. . . . . your neighbours watch TV every day?

   ☐ a) Do

   ☐ b) Does

   ☐ c) Are

13 Lucy

1. Put in the right words

bank, boss, Congratulations, fiancée, foreigner, having, ill, laugh, married, message, news, office, shy, silly, talk, tea, times, typewriter, urgent, wife, worried

Jenny works in a big London (1) . . . . She is a secretary. She is sitting at her (2) . . . . when her friend Vivien comes in.

Vivien: Hello, Jenny, where's Mr Busby, your new (3) . . . .?

Jenny: I don't know. What do you want him for?

Vivien: I've got a (4) . . . . for him from the manager.

Jenny: Is it (5) . . . .?

Vivien: No, it isn't. Tell me, what is Mr Busby like?

Jenny: It's difficult to say. He doesn't (6) . . . . much.

Vivien: People always talk over a cup of (7) . . . . Don't you take him his tea?

Jenny: No, I don't.

Vivien: What? He doesn't want his tea? He must be a (8) . . . .

Jenny: Don't be (9) . . . . Of course he wants his tea. The (10) . . . .-boy makes it.

Vivien: And don't you talk when you're (11) . . . . your tea?

45

Jenny:	No, we don't.
Vivien:	Perhaps he's (12) . . . .
Jenny:	He doesn't look shy.
Vivien:	What does he look like?
Jenny:	He looks (13) . . . .
Vivien:	Is he (14) . . . .?
Jenny:	No.
Vivien:	What is he worrying about, then?
Jenny:	He's worrying about Lucy.
Vivien:	Who is Lucy?
Jenny:	I don't know. Perhaps she is his (15) . . . . He phones and asks how she is several (16) . . . . a day. She must be (17) . . . .

At that moment Mr Busby comes in.

Mr Busby:	Here is good (18) . . . . My Lucy has got three fine babies. All boys.
Jenny:	(19) . . . ., Mr Busby. Do the babies look like you?
Mr Busby:	What are you talking about? Don't make me (20) . . . . Lucy isn't my (21) . . . . She's my dog.

2. Ask questions

Examples:

Where does Lucy work?
(Lucy) She works in a bank.

What do the Browns play?
(the Browns) They play tennis.

1. Where . . . .?
   (these women) They work in Oxford.

2. Where . . . .?
   (your friends) They live in Glasgow.

3. What . . . .?
   (Robert) He smokes cigarettes.

4. Where . . . .?
   (Tom) He comes from Cambridge.

5. What . . . .?
   (Kate) She smokes a pipe.

6. What . . . .?
   (the Smiths) They drink whisky.

7. Where . . . .?
   (the Browns) They come from London.

8. What . . . .?
   (Mr Busby) He is worrying about Lucy.

9. Where . . . .?
   (Jenny and Vivien) They go to a bar.

10. What . . . .?
    (Jack) He is talking about football.

3. Ask questions

Mrs Brown and Mrs Spencer are talking about Mrs Smith's husband:

Mrs Brown: Doesn't he always get up at six o'clock?
Mrs Spencer: No, he never gets up at six o'clock.

1. Mrs Brown: ....?
   Mrs Spencer: No, he never helps in the kitchen.

2. Mrs Brown: ....?
   Mrs Spencer: No, he never makes breakfast.

3. Mrs Brown: ....?
   Mrs Spencer: No, he never makes the beds.

4. Mrs Brown: ....?
   Mrs Spencer: No, he never cleans the floors.

5. Mrs Brown: ....?
   Mrs Spencer: No, he never washes the car.

4. Form new sentences

Examples:

Jenny gets up at six o'clock. (Kate)
Kate doesn't get up at six o'clock.

The Smiths work ten hours. (The Browns)
The Browns don't work ten hours.

1. Freddie plays football. (Jack)
2. Kate likes whisky. (Mary)
3. The Spencers go to bed at eleven o'clock. (The Browns)
4. Jenny goes to work at eight o'clock. (Joy)
5. Roy and Robert work in a bank. (John and Tom)
6. Mr Brown cleans the floors. (Mr Spencer)
7. Mrs Brown drinks tea. (Mrs Spencer)

5. Mark the correct answer with a cross ☒

Examples:

Does Jack like TV? Yes, he . . . . television every day.

☐ a) is watching   ☒ b) watches

What do you want to play? I . . . . tennis.

☒ a) want to play   ☐ b) want play   ☐ c) want playing

1. . . . . want to go to the pub with me? No, I don't.

☐ a) Don't you   ☐ b) Doesn't he   ☐ c) Don't we

2. What does your brother do? He . . . .

☐ a) is playing football.   ☐ b) is a football player.

3. What does a football player do? He . . . .

☐ a) plays football.   ☐ b) is playing football.

4. What . . . .? He plays tennis.

☐ a) does Jack do   ☐ b) Jack does   ☐ c) is Jack doing

5. Where . . . .?

☐ a) does Mary work   ☐ b) Mary works   ☐ c) works Mary

6. Mary . . . . in a bank.

☐ a) work   ☐ b) works

7. Mrs Smith likes tea, but she . . . . like coffee.

☐ a) doesn't   ☐ b) don't

8. Where . . . .? I come from London.

☐ a) do you come from   ☐ b) you come from   ☐ c) come you from

9. Jenny and Vivien . . . . often go to a concert.

☐ a) doesn't   ☐ b) don't   ☐ c) not

10. The Smiths . . . . drink whisky.

☐ a) don't   ☐ b) doesn't   ☐ c) not

14 The Summer Holiday

1. Put in the right words

about, alone, beach, expecting, find, foreign, girl, happy, holidays, kitchen, leaving, next, newspaper, planning, postcard, pubs, sad, son, Spain, staying, travelling, understand

An evening in May. It is raining. Tom Boyd is sitting at the (1) . . . . table, a newspaper in front of him. His mother comes in.

"What are you looking at, Tom?"

"I'm reading (2) . . . . the Costa Brava. That's in (3) . . . . Look at these wonderful pictures in the (4) . . . . I'm going to spend my (5) . . . . . . in Spain this year," says her (6) . . . .

"Why Spain? Why aren't we going to Margate again," asks Mrs Boyd. "It's nice in Margate. We go there every year. Mrs Winter is already (7) . . . . . . us."

"I'm not going to Margate this year, Mother, because I want to see the sun, and I want to find a nice (8) . . . . . . in Spain."

"A (9) . . . . . . girl? What's wrong with British girls?"

"There are lots of British girls on the Costa Brava, Mother. There are even English (10) . . , ... there."

"I can't understand why you're going to Spain to (11) . . . . an English pub. There are plenty of those in Margate. But if you want to go to Spain, let's go. When are we (12) . . . .?"

"Look, Mother, you don't (13) . . . . I'm not going to take you with me this time. I'm (14) . . . . alone. I'm thirty-eight and I want to get a wife. If you're with me all the time, I can't. I'm flying to Spain (15) . . . . month and I'm going to fly (16) . . . ."

"I understand, son, I understand. You don't want your mother with you. It makes me very (17) . . . . I'm going to bed now, Tom. Don't forget to send me a picture (18) . . . . from the Costa Brava. Good night, Tom."

Two months later Mrs Boyd and her son are (19) . . . . in Margate at Mrs Winter's. In the morning they go to the (20) . . . . In the afternoon they play golf, and in the evening they go to a Bingo hall.

Mrs Boyd is (21) . . . . And Tom? He is (22) . . . . to go to Spain next year.

2. Form sentences

What is Mr Spencer going to do?

Example: (get up)
>   He is going to get up.

1. (shave)
2. (clean his shoes)
3. (put on his tie)
4. (read the newspaper)
5. (have breakfast)
6. (drive his car)

3. Form sentences

Tom's Birthday Party
Tom: Hello, Vivien. Can you come to my birthday party next month?
Vivien: Oh, yes. Thank you, Tom. What are we going to do?

Example: Tom: We/eat/ham salad
>   We are going to eat ham salad.

1. We/drink/brandy
2. The girls/make/ice-cream
3. We/dance/rock'n roll
4. We/watch/television
5. The boys/play/table tennis

4. Put in *how, what, when, where, who*

1. . . . . are Kate and Robert going? – They're going to the cinema.

2. . . . . is Mary going next summer? – She's going to Portugal.

3. . . . . is the next bus? – At three o'clock.

4. . . . . is that girl? – It's Kate.

5. Hello, Tom. . . . . are you? – I'm very well, thank you.

6. . . . . are Mrs Smith's children? – Roy and Jenny.

7. . . . . do you come from? – I come from Birmingham.

8. . . . . do you want Mr Busby for? – I've got a message for him.

5. Mark the correct answer with a cross ☒

Example:

Do you . . . . TV every day?
☒ a) watch ☐ b) look

1. Can you . . . . me the way to the Empire State Building?
☐ a) tell ☐ b) say

2. What does Mrs Spencer . . . . in the evening? – She reads the newspaper.
☐ a) do ☐ b) make

3. Robert . . . ., "I'm going to spend my holidays in Portugal this year."
☐ a) tells ☐ b) says

4. Don't you . . . . the office at five o'clock?
☐ a) let ☐ b) leave

5. What is Mr Busby like? – It's difficult to . . . .
☐ a) speak ☐ b) say

6. When does the next train . . . .?
☐ a) live ☐ b) leave

7. What does Freddie . . . .? – He plays football.
☐ a) do ☐ b) make

8. Mr and Mrs Smith . . . . in Brighton, Sussex.
☐ a) live ☐ b) leave

9. Phone Tom, please, and . . . . him that I can't come.
☐ a) tell ☐ b) say

15 On the London-Brighton Road

1. Put in the right words

angry, drink, drive, expensive, faster, fun, increases, larger, less, licences, limit, lunch, never, on, overtake, police, policeman, pubs, red, road, side, wider, wife, wolf, world, worse

Robert and his (1) . . . . Helga are in their car on the London-Brighton (2) . . . .

"We're late," says Robert. "I must drive a little (3) . . . ."

"But there's a speed (4) . . . ., Bob. Why must you go faster than seventy miles an hour?"

"Because I want to be in Brighton for (5) . . . . and because I have a new car. It's bigger and better than the old car."

"It's very (6) . . . ., too," says Helga.

"We have more (7) . . . . . . with it"

"and (8) . . . . . . money for other things," says Helga. "We must have a better television set and a (9) . . . . . . table for the living-room. You spend more money (10) . . . . . . the car than on the house."

"I'm not as bad as that. Other men spend a lot of money in the (11) . . . . That's much (12) . . . . I always say, 'If you drink don't' (13) . . . . . ., if you drive don't (14) . . . .'."

"Be careful, Robert! You're doing eighty-five now."

"I'm as hungry as a (15) . . . . I want to be in Brighton before it's too late for lunch."

"Better late than (16) . . . . Look out! There's a car in front of us."

"That car is doing less than seventy. Let's (17) . . . . it."

"You're the silliest man in the (18) . . . ., Bob. Why don't you wait until the road is (19) . . . .?"

Robert tries to overtake. At that moment the man in the other car (20) . . . . his speed. The two cars race side by (21) . . . . Robert does his best, but his best is not good enough. The other car is faster. Robert is (22) . . . . His face is as (23) . . . . as a tomato. Suddenly a faster car comes from behind and overtakes them both. It stops a little farther down the road. It is a (24) . . . . car. The other two cars must also stop.

"The speed limit is seventy and not ninety," says one (25) . . . . "Your driving-(26) . . . ., please."

2. Opposites

right, upstairs, new, son, good, small, put on

> *Example:*
> hot – cold

		4. wrong	. . . .
1. bad	. . . .	5. take off	. . . .
2. old	. . . .	6. big	. . . .
3. daughter	. . . .	7. downstairs	. . . .

3. Complete the sentences

Kate is fifteen, Jenny is eight, Tom is five, Robert is only two.

Example: Tom is older than Robert.
        Jenny is younger than Kate.

1. Tom . . . . Kate.
2. Kate . . . . Jenny.
3. Jenny . . . . Robert.
4. Robert . . . . Kate.
5. Tom . . . . Jenny.
6. Kate and Jenny . . . . Tom and Robert.
7. Tom and Robert . . . . Kate and Jenny.
8. Robert . . . . Tom.

4. Complete the sentences

Example:

Jack (old) is older than John and Roy. He is the oldest.

1. Roy (young) . . . . John and Jack. He . . . .
2. Jack's hair (long) . . . . John's and Roy's hair. His hair . . . .
3. Roy's hair (short) . . . . Jack's and John's hair. His hair . . . .
4. Jack (big) . . . . John and Roy. He . . . .
5. Roy (small) . . . . Jack and John. He . . . .

5. Mark the correct answer with a cross ☒

Example:

London is . . . . Berlin.

☒ a) bigger than   ☐ b) big as

1. Bobby Fisher is . . . . than Boris Spassky.
   ☐ a) best   ☐ b) better

2. Tom is older than I am. – No, he isn't. He's . . . .
   ☐ a) youngest   ☐ b) younger

3. Mary is a nice girl. – Yes, but Jenny is . . . .
   ☐ a) nicer   ☐ b) nicest

4. Is Vivien happy? – Yes, but Mary is happier . . . . Vivien.
   ☐ a) as   ☐ b) than

5. It's hotter today. – No, it isn't. It's . . . .
   ☐ a) coldest   ☐ b) colder

6. Tom's hair is longer than Robert's and Roy's hair. His hair is . . . .
   ☐ a) longest   ☐ b) the longest

7. Today the weather is . . . . than yesterday.
   ☐ a) bad   ☐ b) worse

8. Robert is younger than Kate, Jenny and Tom. He is . . . .
   ☐ a) the youngest   ☐ b) youngest

9. Who's . . . . player in Glasgow?
   ☐ a) best   ☐ b) the best

10. Mary's got . . . . brothers than I have.
   ☐ a) more   ☐ b) most

16 The Air-Hostess

1. Put in the right words

airport, anything, conductor, difficult, drinks, exciting, expensive, foreign, harder, least, luck, married, most, nationalities, passengers, pleasant, preference, some, tickets, wonderful

It is 10 a.m. A young air-hostess is on the bus to London Airport. The bus (1) . . . . gives her the ticket.

Conductor: Where are you flying today?

Air-hostess: To New York.

Conductor: Some people have all the (2) . . . . You've got the most (3) . . . . job in the world. Can (4) . . . . be more interesting than a day in New York, Berlin or Paris? You stay at the most (5) . . . . hotels and see most wonderful people.

Air-hostess: That's what some people say. It's less (6) . . . . when you do it every day. My job isn't more exciting than your job. We both look after (7) . . . . You give them (8) . . . .; I give them some food, some (9) . . . ., or something to read. There isn't any (10) . . . . job than mine.

Conductor: Do you speak any (11) . . . . languages?

Air-hostess: I speak some French and (12) . . . . German.

Conductor: Who are the most (13) . . . . passengers? Are there any?

Air-hostess: Oh yes, there are some. Babies are the most difficult. They make a lot of work.

Conductor: And which are your most (14) . . . . passengers?

Air-hostess: Young (15) . . . . couples. They don't want anything. They are happy with each other.

Conductor: You meet people of many different (16) . . . . on the plane. Which people do you like best?

Air-hostess: I have no (17) . . . . (She laughs). The Irish drink the (18) . . . ., the Scots spend the (19) . . . . money, and the Americans are the most modest. Well, here's the (20) . . . . Good-bye.

2. Put in *any, anything, some, something*

1. I want . . . . to read. Can I have a newspaper?
2. The young man hasn't got . . . . money.
3. Can . . . . be more interesting than a day in London?
4. There isn't . . . . interesting in the newspaper today.
5. Have you got . . . . books about Brighton?
6. There are . . . . people waiting at the bus stop.
7. The boss doesn't want . . . . tea today.
8. Bring me . . . . butter, please.
9. There isn't . . . . butter in the kitchen.
10. At the bar we can have . . . . nice drinks.

3. Give the answers

Example:

Where's Mary going? (theatre)　　　　　　　She's going to the theatre.

1. Where are the Smiths going? (station)　　. . . . .
2. Where's Bob going? (bank)　　　　　　　. . . . .
3. Where's Jenny going? (airport)　　　　　. . . . .
4. Where's Mr Brown going? (bus stop)　　　. . . . .
5. Where are the Spencers going? (cinema)　. . . . .

4. Ask questions and give answers

Example:

theatre/begin/evening
When does the theatre begin? – The theatre begins in the evening.

1. plane/leave/morning

2. boat/arrive/afternoon

3. boat train/go/evening

4. boat race/begin/morning

5. Mark the correct answer with a cross ☒

Example:

London is . . . . than Manchester.
☐ a) big   ☒ b) bigger   ☐ c) biggest

1. Freddie is a . . . . football player than Bob.
   ☐ a) good   ☐ b) better   ☐ c) best

2. The Smiths have the . . . . house in Brighton.
   ☐ a) large   ☐ b) larger   ☐ c) largest

3. Who's . . . ., Helga or her sister?
   ☐ a) helpful   ☐ b) more helpful   ☐ c) most helpful

4. Isn't your job very interesting, Jenny?
   Oh yes, I've got the . . . . job in the world.
   ☐ a) interesting   ☐ b) more interesting   ☐ c) most interesting

5. Today the weather is . . . . than yesterday.
   ☐ a) bad   ☐ b) worse   ☐ c) worst

6. Is Tom older than Jack? – Yes, but John is the . . . . boy.
   ☐ a) old   ☐ b) older   ☐ c) oldest

7. Which is . . . ., English or German?
   ☐ a) difficult   ☐ b) more difficult   ☐ c) most difficult

8. Which is . . . ., a holiday in New York or a holiday in Brighton?
   ☐ a) expensive   ☐ b) more expensive   ☐ c) most expensive

9. Robert's new car is . . . . than Jenny's old car.
   ☐ a) fast   ☐ b) faster   ☐ c) fastest

10. A bottle of whisky is . . . . than a glass of beer.
    ☐ a) expensive   ☐ b) most expensive   ☐ c) more expensive

17 Something for Nothing

1. Put in the right words

advertisement, alter, beautiful, cry, down, figure, fur, hands, jewellery, leaves, maid, mink, mirror, presents, rushes, selling, speak, suitcase, thief, tomorrow, wears

Dawn Dee, the famous film star, is in her bedroom. She is trying on her (1) . . . . in front of the mirror. The (2) . . . . comes in.

"There's a young man in the hall," she says. He wants to (3) . . . . to you."

"All right. Let him in."

A pleasant young man with a (4) . . . . comes into the room.

"Good evening, madam. I am from Walls and Sons, the furriers of Bond Street. I have a beautiful (5) . . . . coat for you."

"I don't want it. I've got five (6) . . . . coats already. I'm not buying any more."

"But my firm is not (7) . . . . you a fur coat, madam. It's giving one to you. We are not offering fur coats as (8) . . . . to everybody. We're offering one to you, because what Dawn Dee wears today, England (9) . . . . tomorrow. It's an (10) . . . ."

"I understand. But I'm not going to pay a penny for that coat. Is that clear?"

"Yes, madam." – With these words the young man opens his suitcase and shows Miss Dee a (11) . . . . mink coat.

"Oh, what a beautiful coat!" cries Miss Dee. "Oh, give it to me."

He (12) . . . . Dawn Dee the coat. She puts it on and goes to the (13) . . . . Then she walks up and (14) . . . . the room, while the young man is standing at her dressing-table.

"Miss Dee, you've a wonderful (15) . . . . But isn't your fur coat a little too long?"

"Yes," she says. "It's a little too long."

"But we can soon (16) . . . . that. I'm going to take it back to the firm and bring it to you (17) . . . . May I bring some newspaper reporters, too?"

"Of course. Bring as many as you like."

The young man puts the coat back into his suitcase and (18) . . . . the room.

Two minutes later there is a loud (19) . . . ., "Lucy, Lucy!"

The maid (20) . . . . into the room. "What's the matter, Miss Dee?"

"That man's a (21) . . . . He's got my jewellery from the dressing-table."

2. Ask questions

Example:

What does he show Miss Dee?	He shows Miss Dee a fur coat.
Who does he show the coat to?	He shows the coat to Miss Dee.
1. What . . . .?	Jim offers Miss Dee a cigarette.
2. What . . . .?	Miss Dee gives Jim the coat.
3. Who . . . .?	Jim sells the jewellery to Mr Smith.
4. What . . . .?	Mr Smith hands Jim the money.
5. Who . . . .?	Jim shows the coat to Mrs Smith.
6. Who . . . .?	Jim offers the jewellery to Mr Brown.

3. Opposites

dark, happy, left, remember, old, sell, white

Example:

before	–	after	4. buy		. . . .
1. black		. . . .	5. right		. . . .
2. forget		. . . .	6. sad		. . . .
3. light		. . . .	7. young		. . . .

4. Put in *what, where, when, who, why*

1. . . . . is Tom going next summer? He's going to Germany.

2. . . . . is she drinking a cup of tea? Because she's thirsty.

3. . . . . does the young man offer a cup of tea to? He offers a cup of tea to Miss Dee, not to the maid.

4. . . . . are you doing tonight? I'm going to a party.

5. . . . . are you wearing? I'm wearing my red skirt.

6. . . . . are you going? At eight o'clock in the evening.

7. . . . . is Bob? At the bus stop.

8. . . . . is that girl? It's Jane.

9. . . . . must you go faster than seventy miles an hour? Because I want to be in Brighton before lunch.

10. . . . . does the boat train leave? At eight o'clock.

5. Mark the correct answer with a cross ☒

Example:

Jenny works . . . . a big London bank.

☐ a) on   ☒ b) in

1. She works . . . . the fifth floor.

☐ a) on   ☐ b) in

2. Our garden isn't in front of the house. It's . . . . it.

☐ a) after   ☐ b) behind

3. Mrs Smith is waiting . . . . the bus.

☐ a) for   ☐ b) on

4. . . . . are you doing tonight? I'm going to a party.

☐ a) near   ☐ b) next

5. Mary is sitting . . . . her friend.

☐ a) after   ☐ b) behind

6. Tom is watching the news . . . . television.

☐ a) at   ☐ b) on

7. His wife is . . . . the kitchen.

☐ a) in   ☐ b) into

8. Bob goes . . . . bed at ten o'clock.

☐ a) in   ☐ b) to

18 The Cake of Soap (I)

1. Put in the right words

addressed, arrived, at, booked, called, chemist's, clever, continued, dark, evening, feet,
luggage, remembered, searched, soap, stayed, stranger, suit, swindler, tired, worried

Yesterday I walked through Hyde Park in the evening. It was not quite (1) . . . .,
because the street lamps were not far away. I was (2) . . . . and decided to sit on a
bench beside an old gentleman with a dog. I said "Good (3) . . . ." to him, but he
only looked (4) . . . . me and walked away soon afterwards.
Five minutes later a young man (5) . . . . and occupied the old man's seat. He
looked (6) . . . . Suddenly he (7) . . . . me:
"May I tell you what is worrying me? I'm a (8) . . . . here in London."
I had plenty of time and was quite ready to listen.
"I arrived at Paddington Station four hours ago," (9) . . . . the young man. "I
(10) . . . . a taxi and asked the driver to take me to the hotel where I (11) . . . .
two years ago. But that hotel wasn't there any more. The driver showed me another
hotel. I (12) . . . . a room there, changed my (13) . . . ., and then decided to walk
through the streets. As I needed some soap I entered a (14) . . . ., then had a drink
in a pub, and later I looked at the shop windows. Then I wanted to go back to my

hotel, but I (15) .... nothing, neither the name nor the street. The worst is that my money is in my other suit. How can I get a room in another hotel without money and without (16) ....? I'm going to sleep in the park."

I guessed that he wanted money from me. Was he a (17) ....?

"If you can show me that cake of (18) .... from the chemist's," I said, "I can lend you the money for a room."

He (19) .... his pockets, but he hadn't got any soap. Without another word, he jumped to his (20) .... and hurried away. I smiled. I was too (21) .... for him. I decided to go, too. At that moment I stepped on a small packet. I picked it up. It was the cake of soap.

2. Form sentences

Example:

Miss Brown/English/Birmingham/secretary/23
Miss Brown is English.
She comes from Birmingham.
She's a secretary.
She's twenty-three.

1. Miss MacDonald/Scottish/Glasgow/hairdresser/35

2. Freddie Brown/English/London/football player/25

3. John Smith/English/Birmingham/policeman/55

4. Peter Spencer/English/Brighton/postman/41

5. Miss O'Shea/Irish/Dublin/air-hostess/26

3. Put in the correct form of *be*

1. *Tom:* I .... in town yesterday.

2. *Bob:* .... Jenny in town, too?

3. *Tom:* Yes, she ....

4. *Bob:* Where .... you?

5. *Tom:* We .... at the cinema.

6. *Bob:* .... John and Kate at the cinema, too?

7. *Tom:* No, they ....

4. Mark the correct answer with a cross ☒

Example:

Freddie . . . . football every Saturday.

☒ a) plays   ☐ b) play

1. Yesterday I . . . . through Hyde Park in the evening.

    ☐ a) walk   ☐ b) walked

2. . . . . your boss ill yesterday?

    ☐ a) Was   ☐ b) Were

3. Tom's got a car. – Last week he . . . . a car.

    ☐ a) hasn't got   ☐ b) hadn't got

4. I . . . . at home yesterday.

    ☐ a) work   ☐ b) worked

5. I . . . . at the bus stop every day.

    ☐ a) wait   ☐ b) waits

6. Tom . . . . at Paddington Station three hours ago.

    ☐ a) arrives   ☐ b) arrived

7. Bob . . . . the window five minutes ago.

    ☐ a) opens   ☐ b) opened

8. Mr Spencer always . . . . a pipe after supper.

    ☐ a) smokes   ☐ b) smoke

5. Find the same sound

Example:

Tom work**ed** at the bus station last year.

☒ a) look**ed**

☐ b) arriv**ed**

☐ c) continu**ed**

☐ d) smil**ed**

1. Tom arriv**ed** at Paddington Station two hours ago.
   - ☐ a) ask**ed**
   - ☐ b) call**ed**
   - ☐ c) book**ed**
   - ☐ d) walk**ed**

2. Tom wait**ed** for his girl friend yesterday evening.
   - ☐ a) need**ed**
   - ☐ b) help**ed**
   - ☐ c) smok**ed**
   - ☐ d) stepp**ed**

3. Bob wash**ed** the car two hours ago.
   - ☐ a) start**ed**
   - ☐ b) shout**ed**
   - ☐ c) wait**ed**
   - ☐ d) walk**ed**

4. I play**ed** football yesterday.
   - ☐ a) address**ed**
   - ☐ b) walk**ed**
   - ☐ c) help**ed**
   - ☐ d) occupi**ed**

5. Mary hurri**ed** to the bus stop yesterday.
   - ☐ a) continu**ed**
   - ☐ b) wash**ed**
   - ☐ c) help**ed**
   - ☐ d) smok**ed**

19 The Cake of Soap (II)

1. Put in the right words

address, coat, contrary, direction, gave, ground, hard, held, hope, kind, lit, lose, lost, note, showed, something, swindler, took, traffic

I gave a cry of surprise. In my hand I (1) . . . . the proof that the young man was no (2) . . . . I felt very sorry for him. How could I be so (3) . . . .? I couldn't understand my own behaviour. As fast as I could I ran to Hyde Park Corner, but without much (4) . . . .

Suddenly I saw him again. There he stood at the (5) . . . . lights with a sad face. When he saw me he (6) . . . . no sign of pleasure. On the (7) . . . ., he wanted to run away. I caught him and (8) . . . . him the packet.

"I found your cake of soap," I said. "I saw it on the (9) . . . . near the bench. Can I help you with a five-pound (10) . . . .?"

The young man's face suddenly became very happy. He (11) . . . . the packet with the soap and put it in his (12) . . . . pocket.

"You're very (13) . . . . . .," he said. "Thank you very much."

I gave him the five pounds and he thanked me again.

"Here's my card with my (14) . . . .," I said. "Don't (15) . . . . it."

"I'm going to give you back the money as soon as I can, Mr Johnson," he told me and then went off in the (16) . . . . of Piccadilly.

I went back into the park. When I came to my bench, I suddenly stopped. In front of it stood the old gentleman with the dog. He took a match and (17) . . . . it. Then he looked under the seat and behind it. I spoke to him.

"Are you looking for (18) . . . ., sir?" I asked him.

"Yes, a cake of soap. I (19) . . . . it some minutes ago."

2. Give short answers

Jack was in a pub yesterday. Now his mother is very angry.

Example:

Were you there with Mary?   No, I wasn't.

1. Was Jenny there with you?   No, ...
2. Were you there with Helga?   No, ...
3. Were Tom and Robert there?   No, ...
4. Was Bob there with you?   No, ...
5. Was Kate there with you?   No, ...
6. Well, who was with you?   Father . . . .

3. Put in the past tense of the verb

Example:

They played football yesterday. (play)
Tom went to Scotland last month. (go)

1. It was hot, so I . . . . the window. (open)
2. I . . . . dinner with Jenny yesterday. (have)
3. I . . . . Mary in the street yesterday. (see)
4. Helga . . . . to dinner yesterday evening. (come)
5. We . . . . at a very good hotel. (stay)
6. We . . . . about the film for hours. (talk)
7. Ten years ago I . . . . in Brighton. (live)
8. I . . . . the police about the swindler yesterday. (tell)

4. Put in *ago, at, between, in, into, on*

1. Jack walked on the left and Tom on the right. Mary walked . . . . them.

2. I saw Mr Busby . . . . five o'clock today.

3. We went to the theatre . . . . Saturday.

4. Mary was in Germany three weeks . . . .

5. Miss Dee is going . . . . her room.

6. Jenny is . . . . the garden.

5. Mark the correct answer with a cross **X**

Example:

They . . . . football yesterday.
☐ a) play **X** b) played ☐ c) plays

1. We . . . . to Ireland every year.
☐ a) go ☐ b) goes

2. We . . . . in Oxford yesterday.
☐ a) are ☐ b) were

3. You . . . . him in the street yesterday.
☐ a) see ☐ b) saw ☐ c) sees

4. Every morning Mrs Smith . . . . in the house.
☐ a) works ☐ b) work

5. Tom . . . . home at seven o'clock every evening.
☐ a) comes ☐ b) come

6. We . . . . to the cinema yesterday.
☐ a) go ☐ b) went ☐ c) goes

7. She . . . . him at six o'clock yesterday.
☐ a) sees ☐ b) saw ☐ c) see

20 On the Phone

1. Put in the right words

answered, ate, bottle, bunch, cheap, coat, counted, diamond, dinner, home, met, need, Soho, somebody, speaking, spent, station, thirsty, understood, waiter, why, wine, worry

Jim: Hello, Tom, this is Jim (1) . . . . I tried to phone you yesterday evening, but you weren't at (2) . . . .

Tom: No, I wasn't. Didn't you go out yesterday?

Jim: Yes, I did. That's (3) . . . . I'm phoning now.

Tom: Who did you go out with? Did you go out with Ann?

Jim: No, I didn't. I (4) . . . . the most wonderful girl in the world: fur (5) . . . ., (6) . . . . rings, and the rest.

Tom: Where did you go?

Jim: We went to a most expensive restaurant.

Tom: Why didn't you go to a (7) . . . . place in (8) . . . .?

Jim: She wanted to go to that expensive place in the West End. One (9) . . . . showed us to our table, another came with the (10) . . . ., and another one with the (11) . . . . list. She ordered cocktails, caviare and wine. I didn't eat much, but she (12) . . . . for two. At ten o'clock I went to the toilet and (13) . . . . my money. I only had ten pounds in my pocket. I phoned everywhere, but nobody (14) . . . . Everybody was out. It was Saturday, of course. When I went back into the restaurant, there was a (15) . . . . of champagne on the table. She was (16) . . . . Then the flower girl came. I bought a (17) . . . . of flowers. When the bill came, it was fifteen pounds.

Tom: My goodness! What did you do?

Jim: I told her. She said, "I know (18) . . . . not far from here. I'm going to get the money for you. Don't (19) . . . ." I waited and waited, but she didn't come back. At last I called the waiter and told him. First he didn't understand. But when he (20) . . . ., he called the manager and told him.

Tom: What did the manager do?

Jim: He called the police and told them. They took me to the police (21) . . . . where I (22) . . . . the night.

Tom: How did you get out?

Jim: I didn't get out. I'm still at the police station. That's why I'm phoning you. Please come and help me. I (23) . . . . five pounds.

2. Give short answers

Examples:

| Did Mary go to Scotland a year ago? | Yes, she did. |
| Did the Spencers go to Portugal a month ago? | No, they didn't. |

1. Did Jim go to Dublin a year ago?   No, ...
2. Did you play football on Sunday?   No, ...
3. Did the bus arrive late?   Yes, ...
4. Did you and Roy drive to Brighton last year?   No, ...
5. Did Tom spend his holidays in Margate last year?   Yes, ...
6. Did the Smiths have tea in the garden yesterday?   Yes, ...
7. Did Mary go to a pub last night?   No, ...
8. Did your friends go to Scotland last year?   Yes, ...

3. Ask questions

Example:

They (My friends) went to Scotland last year. (Where)
Where did your friends go last year?

1. He (Tom) arrived here last week. (When)

   . . . . here?

2. She (Jenny) said: "No, thanks; I don't smoke." (What)

   . . . .?

3. She (Ann) asked Kate: "Have you any money?" (What)

   . . . .?

4. He (Tom) saw her (Kate) in the street yesterday evening. (Where)

   . . . . yesterday evening?

5. They (The Smiths) had lunch at a restaurant. (Where)

   . . . .?

6. They (The children) played table tennis on Saturday. (When)

   . . . .?

4. Mark the correct answer with a cross ☒

Example:

. . . . did the Smiths arrive? – At half past seven.

☐ a) What   ☒ b) When   ☐ c) Where

1. . . . . Bob come? – Yes, he did.

   ☐ a) Does   ☐ b) Do   ☐ c) Did

2. . . . . the Browns always eat at seven o'clock? –
   No, they sometimes eat at eight o'clock.

   ☐ a) Do   ☐ b) Does   ☐ c) Did

3. Did you dance with Tom? – No, I didn't. I . . . . with Bob.

   ☐ a) dance   ☐ b) danced   ☐ c) dances

4. The dog . . . . my breakfast yesterday.

   ☐ a) eat   ☐ b) ate   ☐ c) eats

5. Jim went out with a girl in a fur coat, he . . . . go out with Ann.
  ☐ a) doesn't   ☐ b) didn't   ☐ c) don't

6. . . . . you play football? – Yes, I do.
  ☐ a) Do   ☐ b) Did   ☐ c) Does

7. Did Tom want apples or oranges? – He . . . . apples.
  ☐ a) wants   ☐ b) wanted   ☐ c) want

8. . . . . you often have coffee for breakfast? – Yes, I do.
  ☐ a) Do   ☐ b) Did   ☐ c) Does

9. . . . . you help your father last summer?
  ☐ a) Do   ☐ b) Did   ☐ c) Does

10. How . . . . Mary feel? – She felt angry.
  ☐ a) does   ☐ b) did   ☐ c) do

11. I . . . . see Tom yesterday, but I saw Bob.
  ☐ a) don't   ☐ b) didn't   ☐ c) doesn't

12. Where . . . . he catch the bus? – He caught it at the theatre.
  ☐ a) does   ☐ b) did   ☐ c) do

5. Mark the correct answer with a cross ☒

Example:

Hello, Jack. Are you waiting for a bus? – No, ...
  ☐ a) I don't   ☒ b) I'm not

Kreisvolkshochschule
Main-Kinzig
645 Hanau, Eugen-Kaiser-Str. 10

1. What's . . . . name? – My name is Tom.
  ☐ a) his   ☐ b) her   ☐ c) your

2. What's Bob wearing? – . . . . wearing a red jacket.
  ☐ a) She's   ☐ b) He's   ☐ c) It's

3. When is the next train? – . . . .
  ☐ a) At four o'clock.   ☐ b) It's five o'clock.   ☐ c) At the station.

4. What's Kate doing? – She's . . . . tea.
  ☐ a) eating   ☐ b) drinking   ☐ c) doing

5. Who is Mr Spencer's . . . . ? – Tom is.
  ☐ a) son   ☐ b) wife   ☐ c) daughter

21 The Guide from London Escort Service

1. Put in the right words

ago, asked, booked, cinema, customer, dress, enjoyed, escort, guide, hall, haven't, on, Palace, rang, restaurant, ring, seen, tired, uniform, walking, Wednesday, work, yet

The phone (1) . . . . in my hotel room. "Your (2) . . . . from *London Escort Service* has just arrived, sir," said the clerk. In the (3) . . . . was a pretty young woman in an air-hostess (4) . . . . Her name was Kitty Baxter.

"Are you going to show me London?" I asked.

"Yes, Herr Fischer," she said. "I am. You've (5) . . . . me for the day until six o'clock. Have you seen the British Museum already?"

"I've never liked museums," I said. "Museums always make me (6) . . . ."

"Have you been to the Tower of London?" she (7) . . . .

"Yes," I said. "I was there two days (8) . . . ., on Thursday."

"Have you ever (9) . . . . Westminster Abbey?"

"No, I haven't seen it (10) . . . . Are you going to take me there first?"

"Yes, if you like," she said. "And after that I'm going to show you the Houses of Parliament and Buckingham (11) . . . ."

We had lunch at a (12) . . . . in the West End.

"I've (13) . . . . every minute so far," I said. "What are we doing this afternoon?"

"Whatever you like," she said. "There's the Zoo in Regent's Park."

"We've done a lot of (14) . . . . this morning," I said. "Is there a good film on in the West End?"

"Yes," she said. "*It Happened on Fridays* is a good film. Have you seen it?"

"No, I (15) . . . . Let's go there."

When we came out of the (16) . . . . it was six o'clock.

"Why didn't we meet last week?" I said. "Can I see you tomorrow?"

"Tomorrow is Sunday," she said. "I never (17) . . . . on Sundays."

"Then I'm going to (18) . . . . your firm and book you for Monday or Tuesday," I said. "I'm leaving on (19) . . . . You've been a perfect guide."

"Thank you, Herr Fischer," she said. "You've been a perfect (20) . . . . Good-bye." On Monday morning the phone rang again. "Your guide from *London Escort Service,* sir," said the clerk. When I came into the hall, I did not trust my eyes. Instead of Kitty Baxter there was a young man in a guide's (21) . . . . "I'm sorry," he said. My wife can't be your (22) . . . . today. Our baby is ill. If you don't mind, I'm going to take you round London."

I didn't enjoy the day half as much as I did (23) . . . . Saturday.

2. Form sentences

At a restaurant

Example:

What have you had, madam?   (grapefruit juice, salad, coffee)
I have had grapefruit juice, salad and coffee.

1. What has Mr Brown had?   (steak and chips, icecream, coffee)
2. What have you had, sir?   (bread and cheese, fruit salad, tomato juice)
3. What have the Spencers had?   (cocktails, caviare, wine)
4. What has Mrs Smith had?   (fish and chips, bread and butter, tea)

3. Questions and answers

Example:

1. Where are you from? – c) I'm from Birmingham.

1. Where are you from?	a) Yes, it is.
2. How are your parents?	b) Yes, I have.
3. Is this your room?	c) I'm from Birmingham.
4. Is there a telephone?	d) Very well, thank you.
5. Where do you work?	e) I work in a bank.
6. Where does your brother work?	f) He works in an office.
7. Does he take the train?	g) Yes, I did.
8. Did you see Tom yesterday?	h) Yes, he does.
9. Was Mary here yesterday?	i) Yes, there is.
10. Have you ever been to Westminster Abbey?	j) Yes, she was.

4. Complete the sentences

Example:

The Smiths sent two invitations yesterday.
But they haven't sent any today.

1. Kate ate three oranges yesterday.

   But . . . . any today.

2. The Browns saw two films yesterday.

   But . . . . any today.

3. Tom read two newspapers yesterday.

   But . . . . any today.

4. Kitty answered three questions yesterday.

   But . . . . any today.

5. Mark the correct answer with a cross ☒

Example:

Two days ago I . . . . the Tower of London.

☐ a) have seen   ☒ b) saw

1. Yesterday I . . . . at the theatre.

☐ a) was   ☐ b) have been

2. Hello, Bob. Did you . . . . a nice holiday?

☐ a) have   ☐ b) had

3. . . . . to New York.

☐ a) I was never   ☐ b) I've never been

4. Why . . . . last week?

☐ a) haven't we met   ☐ b) didn't we meet

5. . . . . you ever seen the British Museum?

☐ a) Did   ☐ b) Have

6. Let's see that exciting film this evening. – But . . . . it already.

☐ a) I saw   ☐ b) I've seen

7. Where did you find this key? – I . . . . it in the garden.

☐ a) have found   ☐ b) found

8. When is Bob going to phone the police? – Oh, ... them already.

☐ a) he phoned   ☐ b) he's phoned

9. Who . . . . in the hotel hall on Monday morning?

☐ a) was   ☐ b) has been

10. Have you ever seen the British Museum? – No, I . . . . it yet.

☐ a) didn't see   ☐ b) haven't seen

22 The Future

1. Put in the right words

big, blond, bright, dark, daughters, engaged, eye, finished, future, glasses, hung, joke,
led, left, marry, money, nose, prefer, pretty, rang, right, sat, sons, tell

The shop window (1) . . . . full of notices. A young man stopped and looked at
them. He read:

> Mrs V. Cummings, 105, Greek Street (1st floor), Soho,
>
> will tell you your (2) . . . .

Five minutes later the young man (3) . . . . at Mrs Cummings's door. A woman
with a sharp (4) . . . . and black eyes opened it and (5) . . . . him to a small
living-room. They both (6) . . . . down at a round table.

"That'll be two pounds," she said and took the (7) . . . . Then she put on her
(8) . . . .

"Let me see your hand, dear. No, no, not the (9) . . . . one. You have to show me
the (10) . . . . hand."

She looked at the young man's hand.

"You'll get a wonderful job," she said. "You'll become the general manager of a

(11) . . . . firm in a year's time. You'll be (12) . . . . to a nice girl in January and (13) . . . . in February. You'll have three daughters, but you won't have any (14) . . . ."

"Will my future wife be (15) . . . .?" asked the young man.

"Gentleman (16) . . . . blonds, but marry what they can get," said the woman with a slight smile on her thin lips. "Your wife will have (17) . . . . hair, but you don't have to worry. She'll be very (18) . . . ."

The young man looked pleased.

"That's fine," he said. "Now may I see your hand, Mrs Cummings?"

"My hand? What for?"

"Well, I'll tell you your future now. You don't have to give me any money, but I think you'll give me back my two pounds when I have (19) . . . ."

"I won't," cried the fortune-teller. "But I can stand a (20) . . . ., if it's a good one. Here's my hand."

"Listen, my good woman, you can't (21) . . . . the future. I married two years ago, my wife is blond, I haven't got any (22) . . . ., but two sons, and I am a policeman. I'm sorry to say that your future won't be very (23) . . . ., if you don't stop this game. Will you give me back my two pounds?"

"Yes, here they are," said Mrs Cummings, and there was no smile on her lips.

"Thank you," said the young policeman. "I'll keep an (24) . . . . on you in future."

2. Questions and answers

Example:

1. Are you George Smith? – c) Yes, I am.

1. Are you George Smith?	a) Yes, it is.
2. Is that your car?	b) Yes, I do.
3. Were you at the office?	c) Yes, I am.
4. Was Mary with you?	d) No, I didn't.
5. Do you always eat at home?	e) Yes, I was.
6. Will you be at home this afternoon?	f) Yes, she has.
7. Did you see Helga yesterday?	g) No, she wasn't.
8. Has she got a car?	h) No, I won't.

3. Put in the right form of the verb

1. Mary always . . . . her mother in the kitchen. (help)

2. I . . . . to a new restaurant yesterday. (go)

3. Please . . . . Mr Busby that I'm here. (tell)

4. I . . . . at five o'clock yesterday. (get up)

5. Tom always . . . . hard every day. (work)

6. He . . . . at home every night. (stay)

7. I . . . . those books home with me last night. (take)

8. He . . . . the house at ten o'clock yesterday morning. (leave)

9. He . . . . to dinner last night. (come)

10. I . . . . now. (get up)

4. Form sentences

Example:

Mary/25/next year
Mary will be twenty-five next year.

1. John/32/tomorrow

2. Mr Brown/57/last year

3. Helga/21/today

4. I/49/next Sunday

5. Mrs Smith/64/yesterday

5. Mark the correct answer with a cross ☒

Example:

Mary . . . . to dinner last night.

☐ a) has come   ☒ b) came

1. Yesterday Jack went to London. Tomorrow he . . . . to Nottingham.

☐ a) will go   ☐ b) went

2. If you give me two pounds, I . . . . you your future.

☐ a) tell   ☐ b) will tell

3. I was tired on Sunday, so I . . . . at ten o'clock.
   ☐ a) have got up   ☐ b) got up

4. We . . . . the film. It was very good.
   ☐ a) liked   ☐ will like

5. They . . . . in London when I was there.
   ☐ a) will be   ☐ b) were

6. Next week I . . . . in New York.
   ☐ a) am   ☐ b) will be

7. Tom and Mary . . . . a party next week.
   ☐ a) will give   ☐ b) give

8. We . . . . to Wales last summer.
   ☐ a) have gone   ☐ b) went

9. Next year Mr Busby . . . . thirty-five.
   ☐ a) will be   ☐ b) was

10. I . . . . out for lunch at twelve o'clock tomorrow.
    ☐ a) will go   ☐ b) went

11. . . . . it rain tomorrow?
    ☐ a) Did   ☐ b) Will

12. . . . . you have dinner at home tomorrow?
    ☐ a) Do   ☐ b) Will

13. If you don't give me two pounds, I . . . . tell you your future.
    ☐ a) didn't   ☐ b) won't

14. He has to close the door, but he . . . . have to close the window.
    ☐ a) don't   ☐ b) doesn't

15. Yesterday I . . . . a bad film.
    ☐ a) saw   ☐ b) have seen

16. Tomorrow Robert . . . . a new car.
    ☐ a) buys   ☐ b) will buy

23 The Hypnotist

1. Put in the right words

aren't, armchair, asleep, awake, began, count, course, don't, didn't, harmless, haven't, nervous, question, selfish, surprise, take, wasn't, weren't, won't, you

When Robert came home one evening, he had a big (1) . . . . . . for Helga.

"I've just finished a (2) . . . . in hypnotism," he said. I'm going to hypnotize you."

Helga was a little (3) . . . . "It's (4) . . . . . ., isn't it?" she asked.

Nevertheless she sat down in an (5) . . . . . ., and Robert (6) . . . . to hypnotize her.

"You are in a deep, deep sleep, Helga. I'll (7) . . . . up to three and you'll open your eyes. You'll answer all my questions, Helga. And you'll tell me the truth, (8) . . . . you? Listen, Helga, listen. One, two, three. Open your eyes now, Helga."

Helga opened her eyes and Robert began to (9) . . . . her.

"I've always been a perfect husband, (10) . . . . I?"

"No, Bob, you haven't. You've always been most (11) . . . ."

"Look here, Helga. I bought you a new car last summer, (12) . . . . I?"

"Who did you buy it for? For me? Don't make me laugh, Bob."

"And your colour TV set? You like it, (13) . . . . you?"

"Yes, I do. But you only bought it because you wanted to see that awful film star Dawn Dee in colour."

"You're joking, (14) . . . . you? Now look here, Helga, our holidays in Scotland last year were wonderful, (15) . . . . they?"

"Who for? For you or for me? You played golf all day. I sat on the beach with the baby. When did I see my dear husband? Only at meals."

"But you love Scotland, don't (16) . . . ., Helga?"

"Of course I do, Bob. But I love the Black Forest more."

At that point Robert did not enjoy his hypnotism any more.

"That will do, Helga, thank you. Wake up now."

"I can't wake up, Bob, darling, because I haven't been (17) . . . . You didn't hypnotize me. I was (18) . . . . all the time. It was a good joke, (19) . . . . it? You're the best and nicest husband in the world, Bob, but you're not a very good hypnotist yet. You must (20) . . . . another course in hypnotism."

2. Fill in the question tags

Example: Mary's a good driver, isn't she?

1. Tom's often been here, ...?
2. The Smiths sat in the garden, ...?
3. Susan went to London yesterday, ...?
4. It's a lovely day, ...?
5. This is your car key, ...?
6. Tom's staying with you next week, ...?
7. You'll stay for dinner, ...?
8. You understand this question, ...?
9. We drank too much whisky, ...?
10. It was a good joke, ...?
11. You love Wales, ...?
12. Robert tried to hypnotize Helga, ...?
13. They'll be late, ...?
14. There'll be four people in the car, ...?
15. You can help me in the kitchen, ...?

3. Put in *how, how many, how much, what, when, where, which, who, whose, why*

1. . . . . books are these? Those books are Mary's.

2. . . . . money has Helga got? Twenty pence.

3. . . . . oranges can she buy? Only four.

4. . . . . does Mr Smith work? He works in an office.

5. . . . . will we do tonight? Let's go to the cinema.

6. . . . . are you going to play? In the park.

7. Hello, Tom. . . . . are you? Fine, thanks.

8. . . . . are you writing to? I'm writing to my sister.

9. . . . . did you call the doctor? Because Susan is ill.

10. . . . . key is this? It's Mary's.

11. . . . . will Helga get here? Tomorrow morning.

12. . . . . hats are those? They're the girls' hats.

13. . . . . are you going to do this afternoon? We're going to play tennis.

4. Mark the correct answer with a cross ☒

Example:

Mr and Mrs Busby stayed . . . . home last Friday.

☐ a) to   ☒ b) at

1. She saw him . . . . five o'clock yesterday.

☐ a) at   ☐ b) on

2. Mrs Smith is going to Liverpool . . . . Friday.

☐ a) at   ☐ b) on

3. She came home . . . . eight o'clock last night.

☐ a) at   ☐ b) on

4. She's going to see him . . . . Sunday morning.

☐ a) on   ☐ b) at

5. We stayed . . . . a very good hotel.

☐ a) at   ☐ b) on

6. Tom Smith and his friend are . . . . the station.

☐ a) on   ☐ b) at

7. Robert is reading . . . . hypnotism.

☐ a) at   ☐ b) about

8. Helga is working . . . . a big import firm.

☐ a) for ☐ b) from

9. Susan is waiting . . . . a phone call.

☐ a) on ☐ b) for

5. Mark the correct answer with a cross ☒

Example:

What's . . . . name? – My name is Jenny.

☐ a) his ☐ b) her ☒ c) your

1. What's Bob wearing? – . . . . wearing a green jacket.

☐ a) He's ☐ b) It's ☐ c) She's

2. Where's Tom? – . . . .

☐ a) At five o'clock. ☐ b) Tomorrow morning. ☐ c) At the bus stop.

3. . . . . Lucy? – She's in the office.

☐ a) Who's ☐ b) Where's ☐ c) What's

4. When is the next plane? – . . . .

☐ a) It's five o'clock. ☐ b) At the airport. ☐ c) At four o'clock.

5. Hello Tom. How are you? – . . . .

☐ a) No, I'm not, thanks. ☐ b) I'm fine, thanks. ☐ c) Yes, I am, thank you.

6. What's Jenny doing? – She's . . . . tea.

☐ a) eating ☐ b) drinking ☐ c) doing

7. Who is Mr Busby's . . . .? – Tom is.

☐ a) daughter ☐ b) wife ☐ c) son

8. Does Mary smoke? – . . . .

☐ a) No, she does. ☐ b) No, she doesn't. ☐ c) Yes, she doesn't.

9. Do you like tea? – Yes, I . . . . drink tea with my breakfast.

☐ a) never ☐ b) always ☐ c) don't

10. . . . . did they arrive? – At ten o'clock.

☐ a) Where ☐ b) What ☐ c) When

11. Is this your umbrella? – No, it's . . . .

☐ a) Tom ☐ b) Tom's ☐ c) Toms

12. . . . . Jenny come? – Yes, she did.

☐ a) Does ☐ b) Do ☐ c) Did

Key to the Exercises

1

Exercise 1

1. Germany 2. German 3. England 4. English 5. invitation 6. holiday 7. way 8. happy 9. station 10. Welcome

Exercise 2

1. Yes, he is. 2. Yes, he is. 3. No, he isn't. 4. Yes, she is. 5. Yes, she is. 6. No, she isn't.

Exercise 3

1. Is Robert German? 2. Is Helga German? 3. Is Robert in Berlin? 4. Is the letter from Robert?

Exercise 4

1. Yes, he is. 2. No, he isn't. 3. Yes, she is. 4. Yes, he is. 5. Yes, it is. 6. No, it isn't. 7. No, she isn't.

Exercise 5

1. d) 2. a) 3. c) 4. a) 5. b)

2

Exercise 1

1. wife 2. supper 3. chips 4. sardines 5. fish 6. plate 7. ham 8. meat 9. egg 10. vegetables 11. butter 12. apples 13. mother 14. cold 15. hot 16. please 17. husband

Exercise 2

1. No, it isn't. It's an apple. 2. No, it isn't. It's a fish. 3. No, it isn't. It's a sausage. 4. No, it isn't. It's an orange.

Exercise 3

1. There are apples. 2. There are fish. 3. There are sausages. 4. There are oranges.

Exercise 4

1. There is . . . . 2. There is . . . . 3. There are . . . . 4. There is . . . . 5. There is . . . . 6. There are . . . . 7. There are . . . . 8. There is . . . .

Exercise 5

1. an 2. a 3. an 4. an 5. a 6. a 7. a 8. a

Exercise 6

1. b) 2. b) 3. d) 4. a) 5. b) 6. a) 7. d)

3

Exercise 1

1. living-room 2. late 3. garden 4. you 5. kitchen 6. dining-room 7. hall 8. upstairs 9. moment 10. God 11. stop 12. bathroom 13. girl 14. cupboard 15. hand

Exercise 2

1. Are the car keys in the hall? 2. Jenny! Where are you? 3. Where are Mr and Mrs Brown? 4. Is Jenny always late? 5. Where are the garden keys?

Exercise 3

1. Yes, I am. 2. No, she isn't. 3. Yes, I am. 4. No, they aren't. 5. Yes, he is. 6. No, it isn't.
7. Yes, we are. 8. No, they aren't.

Exercise 4

1. This is a letter. 2. This is an apple. 3. These are keys. 4. These are letters. 5. These are apples.

Exercise 5

1. That is a ship. 2. That is an orange. 3. Those are plates. 4. Those are ships. 5. Those are oranges.

Exercise 6

1. a) 2. b) 3. a) 4. a) 5. b) 6. a) 7. b) 8. a) 9. b) 10. a)

Exercise 7

1. c) 2. d) 3. a) 4. a) 5. d)

4

Exercise 1

1. luggage 2. sorry 3. booked 4. another 5. guest 6. double 7. outside 8. address 9. kind 10. pleasure 11. call 12. wife 13. today 14. help 15. hall 16. room 17. twin 18. bath 19. key

Exercise 2

1. No, he isn't. He's from Birmingham. 2. Yes, she is. 3. Yes, they are. 4. Yes, it is. 5. Yes, they are. 6. No, it isn't. It's in the hall. 7. Yes, it is.

Exercise 3

1. Is your luggage outside? 2. Is there a guest house in this town? 3. Where's the guest house? 4. Are you Mr and Mrs Brown? 5. Are Mr and Mrs Smith in their room?

Exercise 4

1. Is his name John? No, it isn't, it's Robert. 2. Is her name Jenny? No, it isn't, it's Helga. 3. Is her name Mary? Yes, it is. 4. Is his name Robert? No, it isn't, it's John. 5. Is his name Roy? Yes, it is. 6. Is her name Helga? Yes, it is. 7. Is her name Susan? No, it isn't, it's Linda. 8. Is his name Peter? Yes, it is. 9. Is her name Linda? Yes, it is. 10. Is her name Mary? No, it isn't, it's Susan.

Exercise 5

1. in 2. from 3. in 4. on 5. from 6. on

Exercise 6

1. c) 2. b) 3. b) 4. b) 5. a) 6. a) 7. a) 8. b) 9. b) 10. a)

5

Exercise 1

1. birthday 2. umbrella 3. postman 4. big 5. present 6. ring 7. first 8. Happy 9. lighter 10. guests 11. children 12. girl 13. How 14. me 15. rainy 16. sister 17. kisses 18. you 19. another 20. Guess 21. raincoat

Exercise 2

1. It's on the plate. 2. It's on the table. 3. She's in the kitchen. 4. They're in his hand. 5. He's in the garden. 5. They're on the television set.

Exercise 3

1. Yes, they have. 2. No, I haven't. 3. Yes, they have. 4. Yes, I have. 5. No, they haven't. 6. No, he hasn't. 7. Yes, they have. 8. No, they haven't.

Exercise 4

1. Have you got a raincoat? No, I haven't. 2. Has Helga got an umbrella? Yes, she has. 3. Have you got a cigarette-lighter? Yes, I have. 4. Have your neighbours got a television set? No, they haven't. 5. Have the Smiths got two children? Yes, they have. 6. Have they got a garden? Yes, they have.

Exercise 5

1. b) 2. a) 3. b) 4. b) 5. b) 6. a) 7. a) 8. a) 9. a)

6

Exercise 1

1. phone 2. order 3. Herrings 4. chickens 5. figs 6. pigs 7. quality 8. bears 9. pears 10. beer 11. noodles 12. grapes 13. line 14. raincoat 15. present 16. hams 17. sheep 18. tins 19. sauerkraut

Exercise 2

1. What's his name? 2. What's your name? 3. What's your address? 4. Is her name Mary? 5. What's her name?

Exercise 3

1. twenty 2. six 3. eight 4. twelve 5. four 6. nine 7. two 8. fifteen 9. nineteen 10. eleven

Exercise 4

1. There are two oranges on the plate. 2. There are four oranges on the plate. 3. There is one apple on the table. 4. There are five apples on the table. 5. There is one girl at the bus stop. 6. There are six girls at the bus stop. 7. There are three parcels in the cupboard. 8. There are eight parcels in the cupboard.

Exercise 5

1. b) 2. a) 3. b) 4. a) 5. a) 6. b) 7. a) 8. c) 9. a) 10. b) 11. a)

7

Exercise 1

1. ring 2. Answer 3. speaking 4. neighbour 5. watching 6. upstairs 7. living-room 8. Lock 9. locked 10. for 11. man 12. together 13. police 14. helping 15. bedroom 16. broken 17. beside

Exercise 2

1. What's your name? 2. How are you? 3. Where's John? 4. How is he today? 5. Is this your lighter? 6. Where's my raincoat? 7. Has Jenny got a phone? 8. What's her number?

Exercise 3

1. What 2. Where 3. What 4. Who 5. Where 6. What

Exercise 4

1. What is Robert doing? He is sitting in the living-room. 2. What is Helga doing? She is watching TV. 3. What is Vivien doing? She is phoning Robert. 4. What is Robert doing? He is going to Vivien's house. 5. What is the policeman doing? He is watching Robert. 6. What is the cat doing? It is sitting on the floor. 7. What are Robert and Helga doing? They are waiting at the bus stop. 8. What are Robert and Helga doing? They are hurrying to the station. 9. What are Robert and Helga doing? They are going to Germany. 10. What are Mr and Mrs Brown doing? They are locking their car. 11. What are the Browns doing? They are going to their house. 12. What are the Browns doing? They are watching TV.

Exercise 5

1. What is Joy doing? She's watching TV. 2. What is Robert doing? He's phoning the police. 3. What are the children doing? They're helping a neighbour. 4. What is the policeman doing? He's watching John. 5. What is the girl doing? She's sitting on the floor. 6. What are the boys doing? They're hurrying to the station.

Exercise 6

1. What is Robert doing? Is he calling the police?
   No, he isn't. He is answering the phone.
2. What is Vivien doing? Is she watching TV?
   No, she isn't. She is phoning from the living-room.
3. What is the man doing? Is he ringing at the door?
   No, he isn't. He is moving upstairs.
4. What is Helga doing? Is she locking the door?
   No, she isn't. She is phoning the police.
5. What is the policeman doing? Is he watching the house?
   No, he isn't. He is hurrying upstairs.
6. What is the cat doing? Is it having a meal?
   No, it isn't. It is sitting on the floor.

8

Exercise 1

1. for 2. Wait 3. holds 4. lady 5. lift 6. floor 7. sixth 8. stops 9. stuck 10. ticket 11. theatre 12. Press 13. rings 14. fifth 15. happens 16. spoilt 17. name 18. button 19. third 20. reaches 21. evening 22. idea

Exercise 2

1. in 2. for 3. on 4. at 5. to

Exercise 3

1. waits 2. watch 3. helps 4. wait 5. goes 6. watches 7. help 8. go

Exercise 4

1. b) 2. a) 3. b) 4. b) 5. b) 6. a)

Exercise 5

1. a) 2. c) 3. d) 4. a) 5. c)

9

Exercise 1

1. hairdresser's 2. set 3. already 4. date 5. waits 6. hour 7. minutes 8. quarter 9. late 10. at 11. lend 12. wig 13. disappears 14. leaves 15. quarters 16. past 17. statue 18. clock 19. terrible 20. watch 21. addresses 22. time 23. surprise

Exercise 2

1. It's eight o'clock. 2. It's ten past eight. 3. It's a quarter past eight. 4. It's half past eight. 5. It's a quarter to nine. 6. It's ten to nine. 7. It's one minute to nine. 8. It's three o'clock.

Exercise 3

1. Where are you going?   I'm going to Berlin.
   Who's going with you?   My sister is.
   When are you going?   At twenty past eleven.

2. Where are you going?   I'm going to London.
   Who's going with you?   My wife is.
   When are you going?   At a quarter to eleven.

3. Where are you going?   I'm going to Birmingham.
   Who's going with you?   My mother is.
   When are you going?   At a quarter past nine.

4. Where are you going?   I'm going to Glasgow.
   Who's going with you?   My daughter is.
   When are you going?   At five to ten.

5. Where are you going?   I'm going to Germany.
   Who's going with you?   My husband is.
   When are you going?   At a quarter to nine.

Exercise 4

1. At ten past eight John and Kate are still in the lift.
2. At a quarter past eight a voice says: "Press the button."
3. At half past eight they have a drink in the bar.
4. At a quarter to eleven they are still in the bar.
5. At eleven o'clock they are in the lift again.

Exercise 5

c) e) g) h)

Exercise 6

1. enters 2. gives 3. are waiting 4. calls 5. am doing 6. leaves 7. hurries 8. are waiting 9. doing 10. is addressing

10

Exercise 1

1. reporter 2. questions 3. train 4. Saturday 5. play 6. Sunday 7. read 8. page 9. favourite 10. drink 11. smoke 12. pipe 13. watch 14. sitting 15. playing 16. answering 17. reading 18. drinking 19. having 20. smoking 21. watching 22. giving

Exercise 2

1. He always leaves his house at eight o'clock. 2. At ten o'clock he answers the reporters questions. 3. He trains very hard in the evening. 4. He often drinks a glass of beer. 5. He always reads the sports page. 6. He sometimes smokes a pipe. 7. He has supper at half past seven every evening. 8. He often watches football on TV.

Exercise 3

1. Robert always reads the newspaper in the evening. 2. The boys often play football on Saturdays. 3. He sometimes leaves the house at six o'clock. 4. He seldom helps his wife in the kitchen. 5. Robert always smokes a pipe after supper. 6. Tom never drinks whisky in the morning.

Exercise 4

1. go 2. wife 3. never 4. answer 5. mother 6. boy 7. get out 8. seldom 9. evening

Exercise 5

1. c) 2. b) 3. b) 4. c) 5. a) 6. b) 7. c)

11

Exercise 1

1. arrive 2. hungry 3. single 4. floor 5. lift 6. walk 7. gentlemen 8. restaurant 9. meal 10. start 11. ground 12. tell 13. begins 14. end 15. must 16. until 17. turn 18. cannot 19. can 20. short 21. downstairs

Exercise 2

1. j) 2. c) 3. a) 4. d) 5. f) 6. e) 7. b) 8. g) 9. h) 10. i)

Exercise 3

1. Miss Kate Winter
    25 Grimston Gardens
    Folkestone
    Kent
    England

2. Mr Jack Quick
    40 Shaftesbury Avenue
    London, W1V 8HJ
    England

3. Mr and Mrs Robert Smith
    33 Palmeira Mansions
    Hove
    Sussex
    England

4. Mr John Blake
    14 Durlston Road
    Poole
    Dorset
    England

Exercise 4

1. No, we can't. 2. Yes, you must. 3. Yes, he can. 4. No, she can't. 5. Yes, they must. 6. No, you (we) may not. 7. Yes, you may. 8. No, she may not. 9. No, he can't.

Exercise 5

1. May I have a glass of beer? 2. Can we have a double room? 3. Must the men walk up? 4. Can you play tennis? 5. May John watch TV?

Exercise 6

1. a) 2. a) 3. b) 4. a) 5. b) 6. b) 7. a) 8. b) 9. a) 10. a) 11. a) 12. b) 13. b) 14. a)

12

Exercise 1

1. on 2. never 3. boss 4. always 5. play 6. help 7. her 8. home 9. washing 10. ask 11. take 12. doctor 13. spend 14. friend 15. drive 16. car 17. office 18. welcome 19. notice 20. answers 21. lucky 22. liar

Exercise 2

1. i) 2. a) 3. d) 4. c) 5. b) 6. h) 7. e) 8. f) 9. g)

Exercise 3

1. He seldom reads the newspaper. 2. She sometimes washes the car. 3. They often dance. 4. He never plays football. 5. They sometimes play tennis. 6. She never smokes a pipe. 7. She seldom drinks whisky.

Exercise 4

1. No, he doesn't. 2. Yes, they do. 3. No, they don't. 4. No, she doesn't. 5. Yes, he does. 6. Yes, she does. 7. No, he doesn't. 8. Yes, they do.

Exercise 5

1. b) 2. b) 3. a) 4. c) 5. b) 6. c) 7. a)

13

Exercise 1

1. bank 2. typewriter 3. boss 4. message 5. urgent 6. talk 7. tea 8. foreigner 9. silly 10. office 11. having 12. shy 13. worried 14. married 15. fiancée 16. times 17. ill 18. news 19. Congratulations 20. laugh 21. wife

Exercise 2

1. Where do these women work? 2. Where do your friends live? 3. What does Robert smoke? 4. Where does Tom come from? 5. What does Kate smoke? 6. What do the Smiths drink? 7. Where do the Browns come from? 8. What is Mr Busby worrying about? 9. Where do Jane and Vivien go? 10. What is Jack talking about?

Exercise 3

1. Doesn't he always help in the kitchen? 2. Doesn't he always make breakfast? 3. Doesn't he always make the beds? 4. Doesn't he always clean the floors? 5. Doesn't he always wash the car?

Exercise 4

1. Jack doesn't play football. 2. Mary doesn't like whisky. 3. The Browns don't go to bed at eleven o'clock. 4. Joy doesn't go to work at eight o'clock. 5. John and Tom don't work in a bank. 6. Mr Spencer doesn't clean the floors. 7. Mrs Spencer doesn't drink tea.

Exercise 5

1. a) 2. b) 3. a) 4. a) 5. a) 6. b) 7. a) 8. a) 9. b) 10. a)

14

Exercise 1

1. kitchen 2. about 3. Spain 4. newspaper 5. holidays 6. son 7. expecting 8. girl 9. foreign 10. pubs 11. find 12. leaving 13. understand 14. travelling 15. next 16. alone 17. sad 18. postcard 19. staying 20. beach 21. happy 22. planning

Exercise 2

1. He is going to shave. 2. He is going to clean his shoes. 3. He is going to put on his tie. 4. He is going to read the newspaper. 5. He is going to have breakfast. 6. He is going to drive his car.

Exercise 3

1. We are going to drink brandy. 2. The girls are going to make ice-cream. 3. We are going to dance rock n'roll. 4. We are going to watch television. 5. The boys are going to play table tennis.

Exercise 4

1. Where 2. Where 3. When 4. Who 5. How 6. Who 7. Where 8. What

Exercise 5

1. a) 2. a) 3. b) 4. b) 5. b) 6. b) 7. a) 8. a) 9. a)

15

Exercise 1

1. wife 2. road 3. faster 4. limit 5. lunch 6. expensive 7. fun 8. less 9. larger 10. on 11. pubs 12. worse 13. drive 14. drink 15. wolf 16. never 17. overtake 18. world 19. wider 20. increases 21. side 22. angry 23. red 24. police 25. policeman 26. licences

Exercise 2

1. good 2. new 3. son 4. right 5. put on 6. small 7. upstairs

Exercise 3

1. Tom is younger than Kate. 2. Kate is older than Jenny. 3. Jenny is older than Robert. 4. Robert is younger than Kate. 5. Tom is younger than Jenny. 5. Kate and Jenny are older than Tom and Robert. 7. Tom and Robert are younger than Kate and Jenny. 8. Robert is younger than Tom.

Exercise 4

1. Roy is younger than John and Jack. He is the youngest. 2. Jack's hair is longer than John's and Roy's hair. His hair is the longest. 3. Roy's hair is shorter than Jack's and John's hair. His hair is the shortest. 4. Jack is bigger than John and Roy. He is the biggest. 5. Roy is smaller than Jack and John. He is the smallest.

Exercise 5

1. b) 2. b) 3. a) 4. b) 5. b) 6. b) 7. b) 8. a) 9. b) 10. a)

16

Exercise 1

1. conductor 2. luck 3. wonderful 4. anything 5. expensive 6. exciting 7. passengers 8. tickets 9. drinks 10. harder 11. foreign 12. some 13. difficult 14. pleasant 15. married 16. nationalities 17. preference 18. least 19. most 20. airport

Exercise 2

1. something 2. any 3. anything 4. anything 5. any 6. some 7. any 8. some 9. any 10. some

Exercise 3

1. They're going to the station. 2. He's going to the bank. 3. She's going to the airport.
4. He's going to the bus stop. 5. They're going to the cinema.

Exercise 4

1. When does the plane leave? – The plane leaves in the morning.
2. When does the boat arrive? – The boat arrives in the afternoon.
3. When does the boat train go? – The boat train goes in the evening.
4. When does the boat race begin? – The boat race begins in the morning.

Exercise 5

1. b) 2. c) 3. b) 4. c) 5. b) 6. c) 7. b) 8. b) 9. b) 10. c)

17

Exercise 1

1. jewellery 2. maid 3. speak 4. suitcase 5. mink 6. fur 7. selling 8. presents 9. wears 10. advertisement 11. beautiful 12. hands 13. mirror 14. down 15. figure 16. alter 17. tomorrow 18. leaves 19. cry 20. rushes 21. thief

Exercise 2

1. What does Jim offer Miss Dee? 2. What does Miss Dee give Jim? 3. Who does Jim sell the jewellery to? 4. What does Mr Smith hand Jim? 5. Who does Jim show the coat to? 6. Who does Jim offer the jewellery to?

Exercise 3

1. white 2. remember 3. dark 4. sell 5. left 6. happy 7. old

Exercise 4

1. Where 2. Why 3. Who 4. What 5. What 6. When 7. Where 8. Who 9. Why 10. When

Exercise 5

1. a) 2. b) 3. a) 4. a) 5. b) 6. b) 7. a) 8. b)

18

Exercise 1

1. dark 2. tired 3. evening 4. at 5. arrived 6. worried 7. addressed 8. stranger 9. continued 10. called 11. stayed 12. booked 13. suit 14. chemist's 15. remembered 16. luggage 17. swindler 18. soap 19. searched 20. feet 21. clever

Exercise 2

1. Miss MacDonald is Scottish. She comes from Glasgow. She's a hairdresser. She's thirty-five. 2. Freddie Brown is English. He comes from London. He's a football player. He's twenty-five. 3. John Smith is English. He comes from Birmingham. He's a policeman. He's fifty-five. 4. Peter Spencer is English. He comes from Brighton. He's a postman. He's forty-one. 5. Miss O'Shea is Irish. She comes from Dublin. She's an air-hostess. She's twenty-six.

Exercise 3

1. was 2. was 3. was 4. were 5. were 6. were 7. weren't

Exercise 4

1. b) 2. a) 3. b) 4. b) 5. a) 6. b) 7. b) 8. a)

Exercise 5

1. b) 2. a) 3. d) 4. d) 5. a)

19

Exercise 1

1. held 2. swindler 3. hard 4. hope 5. traffic 6. showed 7. contrary 8. gave 9. ground 10. note 11. took 12. coat 13. kind 14. address 15. lose 16. direction 17. lit 18. something 19. lost

Exercise 2

1. No, she wasn't. 2. No, I wasn't. 3. No, they weren't. 4. No, he wasn't. 5. No, she wasn't. 6. Father was.

Exercise 3

1. opened 2. had 3. saw 4. came 5. stayed 6. talked 7. lived 8. told

Exercise 4

1. between 2. at 3. on 4. ago 5. into 6. in

Exercise 5

1. a) 2. b) 3. b) 4. a) 5. a) 6. b) 7. b)

20

Exercise 1

1. speaking 2. home 3. why 4. met 5. coat 6. diamond 7. cheap 8. Soho 9. waiter 10. dinner 11. wine 12. ate 13. counted 14. answered 15. bottle 16. thirsty 17. bunch 18. somebody 19. worry 20. understood 21. station 22. spent 23. need

Exercise 2

1. No, he didn't. 2. No, I didn't. 3. Yes, it did. 4. No, we didn't. 5. Yes, he did. 6. Yes, they did. 7. No, she didn't. 8. Yes, they did.

Exercise 3

1. When did Tom arrive here? 2. What did Jenny say? 3. What did Ann ask Kate? 4. Where did Tom see Kate yesterday evening? 5. Where did the Smiths have lunch? 6. When did the children play table tennis?

Exercise 4

1. c) 2. a) 3. b) 4. b) 5. b) 6. a) 7. b) 8. a) 9. b) 10. b) 11. b) 12. b)

Exercise 5

1. c) 2. b) 3. a) 4. b) 5. a)

21

Exercise 1

1. rang 2. guide 3. hall 4. dress 5. booked 6. tired 7. asked 8. ago 9. seen 10. yet 11. Palace 12. restaurant 13. enjoyed 14. walking 15. haven't 16. cinema 17. work 18. ring 19. Wednesday 20. customer 21. uniform 22. escort 23. on

Exercise 2

1. He has had steak and chips, ice-cream and coffee. 2. I have had bread and cheese, fruit salad and tomato juice. 3. They have had cocktails, caviare and wine. 4. She has had fish and chips, bread and butter, and tea.

Exercise 3

1. c) 2. d) 3. a) 4. i) 5. e) 6. f) 7. h) 8. g) 9. j) 10. b)

Exercise 4

1. she hasn't eaten 2. they haven't seen 3. he hasn't read 4. she hasn't answered

Exercise 5

1. a) 2. a) 3. b) 4. b) 5. b) 6. b) 7. b) 8. b) 9. a) 10. b)

22

Exercise 1

1. hung 2. future 3. rang 4. nose 5. led 6. sat 7. money 8. glasses 9. right 10. left 11. big 12. engaged 13. marry 14. sons 15. blond 16. prefer 17. dark 18. pretty 19. finished 20. joke 21. tell 22. daughters 23. bright 24. eye

Exercise 2

1. c) 2. a) 3. e) 4. f) 5. b) 6. h) 7. d) 8. f)

Exercise 3

1. helps 2. went 3. tell 4. got up 5. works 6. stays 7. took 8. left 9. came 10. am getting up

Exercise 4

1. John will be thirty-two tomorrow. 2. Mr Brown was fifty-seven last year. 3. Helga is twenty-one today. 4. I will be forty-nine next Sunday. 5. Mrs Smith was sixty-four yesterday.

Exercise 5

1. a) 2. b) 3. b) 4. a) 5. b) 6. b) 7. a) 8. b) 9. a) 10. a) 11. b) 12. b) 13. b) 14. b) 15. a) 16. b)

23

Exercise 1

1. surprise 2. course 3. nervous 4. harmless 5. armchair 6. began 7. count 8. won't 9. question 10. haven't 11. selfish 12. didn't 13. don't 14. aren't 15. weren't 16. you 17. asleep 18. awake 19. wasn't 20. take

Exercise 2

1. hasn't he 2. didn't they 3. didn't she 4. isn't it 5. isn't it 6. isn't he 7. won't you 8. don't you 9. didn't we 10. wasn't it 11. don't you 12. didn't he 13. won't they 14. won't there 15. can't you

Exercise 3

1. Whose 2. How much 3. How many 4. Where 5. What 6. Where 7. how 8. Who 9. Why 10. Whose 11. when 12. Whose 13. What

Exercise 4

1. a) 2. b) 3. a) 4. a) 5. a) 6. b) 7. b) 8. a) 9. b)

Exercise 5

1. a) 2. c) 3. b) 4. c) 5. b) 6. b) 7. c) 8. b) 9. b) 10. c) 11. b) 12. c)

English for All, Teil 1

Klett-Nummer

	Klett-Nummer
Lehrbuch für den Kursteilnehmer, 147 S.	5244
Lehrerheft, 48 S.	52443
Workbook 1 Lesson 1–23	52445
4 Schallplatten, 17 cm ∅, 33 U/min Reading-Texts and Dialogues	52441
3 Schallplatten, 17 cm ∅, 33 U/min Structural Exercises mit Arbeitsheft	52442
Compact-Cassette, Reading-Texts and Dialogues, complete with pauses for repetition (Lehrerspur besprochen)	99521
Compact-Cassette, Structural Exercises, mit Arbeitsheft (beide Halbspuren besprochen)	53447
Tonband, Reading-Texts and Dialogues, 9,5 cm/sec complete with pauses for repetition (erste Halbspur besprochen)	99520
Tonband, Structural Exercises, 9,5 cm/sec mit Arbeitsheft (beide Halbspuren besprochen)	52449

Labormaterialien
Structural Exercises for Beginners

Programmtexte Lesson 1–23, 141 S.	99517
1 Satz Tonbänder, Sprechzeit 5 h, 10 min, 9,5 cm/sec (erste Halbspur besprochen)	99518
1 Satz Compact-Cassetten (Lehrerspur besprochen)	99519

Tests

Testaufgaben zu Lesson 1–23	52471

fehler abc

Deutsch-Englisch

von Heinz Gildhoff

Klettbuch 51851

Fehler sind nicht besonders originell. Es werden nämlich immer die gleichen gemacht:

80% aller Fehler beim Gebrauch der englischen Sprache lassen sich auf 99 „problematische" Wörter und Begriffe zurückführen. Das haben sorgfältige Fehleranalysen und statistische Unterlagen bewiesen.

Die 99 Fehlerquellen werden im Fehler-ABC Deutsch-Englisch behandelt. Die Wörter und Ausdrücke sind erklärt und mit Übersetzungs- und Anwendungsbeispielen versehen.

50 Kontrollaufgaben am Anfang des Buches zeigen dem Lernenden seine typischen Fehler. Mit dem Fehler-ABC kann er sie gezielt bekämpfen. Eine Anleitung hilft ihm dabei.

 Klett